Making Sense of Spelling and Pronunciation

Christine Digby

John Myers

Prentice Hall

New York   London   Toronto   Sydney   Tokyo   Singapore

PRENTICE HALL INTERNATIONAL ENGLISH LANGUAGE TEACHING

First published 1993 by
Prentice Hall International (UK) Ltd
Campus 400, Maylands Avenue
Hemel Hempstead
Hertfordshire HP2 7EZ
A division of
Simon & Schuster International Group

Typeset in 10/12pt Palatino and 11/13pt Gill Sans Light
by Goodfellow & Egan Phototypesetting Ltd, Cambridge

Printed and bound in Great Britain by The Bath Press, Avon

Illustrations by Harry Venning & PanTex Arts

Library of Congress Cataloging-in-Publication Data

Digby, Christine.
    Making sense of spelling and pronunciation/Christine Digby,
John Myers.
        p.   cm.
    ISBN 0-13-554205-7 : $9.00 (U.S.)
    1. English language--Orthography and spelling--Study and
teaching.   2. English language--Pronunciation--Study and
teaching.   I. Myers, John   II. Title.
    [LB1574.D54   1992]
372.6'32--dc20   92-23301
                                                              CIP

British Library Cataloguing in Publication Data

A catalogue record for this book is available from the British
Library.

    ISBN 0-13-554205-7   (pbk)
    ISBN 0-13-554197-2   (pbk)   *Self Study*

1 2 3 4 5   96 95 94 93

Contents

Introduction

To the student

How many times have you had problems with spelling and pronunciation of English words? How many times have you wished there was a book that gave you help with words that you have heard but are not sure how to spell? Or words that you can write but don't know how to say? *Making Sense of Spelling and Pronunciation* has been written to help you understand the rules and patterns of everyday English words.

When there is an easy rule we have given it to you. When there isn't, we have given you examples of some of the common words that you are likely to find and need in everyday situations.

But this isn't just a book of rules and word lists. What you need is practice so you can learn and remember the most common patterns in spelling and pronunciation. Sometimes we give you the rule and then let you test your understanding in practical exercises. Sometimes we show you the most common examples and then give you practice in using them.

Making Sense of Spelling and Pronunciation is divided into two sections. In Part 1 we show you the different ways of spelling the sounds of English. Have you ever thought of how many ways there are of spelling the sound /i:/, for example? Is it only **ee** as in *sheep* or **ea** as in *cheap*? Look at the first page of Part 1 to find out. Then do the puzzle that follows, to find more examples of the different spellings for this sound in English.

In Part 2 of the book we look at the different ways of pronouncing English words. We can't tell you *why* we don't always pronounce the same letters in the same way, but we can help you to learn the simplest rules and patterns for most of the words you will need in everyday life. For example, in Unit 2 of Part 2, you will learn about the letter **a** at the beginning of a word. Is it always pronounced /æ/ as in *animal*? Once you have studied all the ways of pronouncing **a** you can turn to the 'Practice' section and test what you have learnt by labelling the pictures and matching words to their definitions and then answering questions about their pronunciation.

We hope that you will find this book interesting and useful.

To the teacher

English is a notoriously difficult language to spell and pronounce. Students are often bewildered by the seemingly anarchic sound/spelling system of English. There often seem to be more exceptions than rules, and the mastery of accurate spelling and correct pronunciation sometimes seems a daunting and demotivating task.

This book does not claim to cover all the rules, or all the exceptions to those rules, but it does go some way towards finding order in chaos. By giving students practice in recognising and using the rules, it reinforces some of the patterns which underlie English spelling and pronunciation as well as focusing on the words students frequently have problems with.

Part 1 deals with the different ways in which sounds can be spelt. Part 2 deals with ways in which spelling patterns are pronounced as sounds. The book is organised not as a sequence of lessons but in an order that will make it easy for both teacher and student to find relevant sections. So, for example, the rules for pronouncing initial vowels are placed together at the beginning of Part 2. In the Self Study edition there is an answer key at the end of the book.

The book can be used in two main ways. In the classroom teachers may use it as a reference for the rules and patterns and as a source of exercises and activities. Or the Self Study edition can be used as a self-access book – students can discover the rules and patterns for themselves and then test their knowledge by doing the exercises and checking their answers in the key.

Making Sense of Spelling and Pronunciation is also a useful aid for teachers who wish to introduce and practise the use of the phonetic alphabet with their classes. We include a phonetic chart of the symbols used throughout the book.

Phonetic chart

Vowels

Short vowels		*Long vowels*		*Dipthongs*	
æ	(bat)	ɑː	(dark)	eɪ	(say)
e	(bet)	iː	(seem)	aɪ	(buy)
ə	(ago)	ɔː	(born)	ɔɪ	(toy)
ɪ	(sit)	ɜː	(term)	əʊ	(so)
ɒ	(top)	uː	(moon)	aʊ	(now)
ʌ	(but)			ɪə	(peer)
ʊ	(put)			eə	(fair)
				ʊə	(poor)

Consonants

b	(big)	n	(no)	ʃ	(ship)
d	(dog)	p	(pot)	tʃ	(church)
f	(fat)	r	(rose)	ʒ	(measure)
g	(go)	s	(sit)	dʒ	(jet)
h	(hand)	t	(tap)	j	(yes)
k	(kite)	v	(very)	ŋ	(long)
l	(lip)	w	(week)	θ	(thin)
m	(milk)	z	(zoo)	ð	(these)

Glossary of terms

auxiliary verb	a verb used with a main verb to form questions and negatives, to form tenses and to show mood (*eg: Does* she live here? I *have* seen her. I *must* see her.)
consonants	all letters which are not vowels: **b c d f g h j k l m n p q r s t v w x y z**
dipthong	the sound made when one syllable contains two vowel sounds (*eg*: make /meɪk/, near /nɪə/)
final letter	the last letter of a word (*eg*: the final letter of *student* is **t**)
initial letter	the first letter of a word (*eg*: the initial letter of *student* is **s**)
prefix	one or more syllables added to the beginning of a word to change its meaning (*eg*: known – unknown)
rhyme	the same sound in two or more words or syllables (*eg*: prudent student, clear beer)
stress	extra emphasis or force used when saying a particular word or syllable (*eg*: in *student* the stress is on the first syllable: stúdent)
suffix	one or more syllables added to the end of a word to change its meaning or grammatical function (*eg*: quick – quickly)
syllables	the units of sound into which words are broken (*eg*: *student* has two syllables – stu dent)
unvoiced sounds	/f/ /k/ /h/ /p/ /t/ /tʃ/ /θ/ /s/ /ʃ/
voiced sounds	can be identified by placing your finger on your throat while saying these sounds: if you can feel vibrations, the phoneme is voiced. All vowels and dipthongs and also the following phonemes: /b/ /d/ /g/ /v/ /n/ /m/ /ŋ/ /r/ /j/ /v/ /z/ /dʒ/ /ð/ /l/
vowels	the letters: **a e i o u**

Part 1: Spelling

I

/iː/

The sound /iː/ can be spelt in many ways. The easiest to remember are:

ee (*eg*: sheep succeed)
ea (*eg*: cream cheap)

But there are also other ways to spell /iː/:

e + consonant + **e** (*eg*: scene complete)
i + consonant + **e** (*eg*: chlorine elite)
ie (*eg*: thief niece handkerchief)
ei (*eg*: ceiling conceit receipt)

Trying to remember whether to use **ie** or **ei** to spell /iː/ gives everyone problems, but there is a simple rule:

i before **e**
except after **c**

> **But be careful!**
> There are exceptions to this rule (*eg*: fancied protein).

PRACTICE

1 Find all the words with the sound /ɪː/ in this puzzle.

```
S  C  H  E  M  E  E  X  S  D
W  A  E  A  M  B  V  R  T  R
E  N  A  T  H  L  E  T  E  E
E  T  T  E  A  C  H  Z  A  A
T  E  A  M  P  F  E  E  L  M
Q  E  M  A  C  H  I  N  E  Q
V  N  K  R  S  E  A  T  G  U
R  A  V  I  N  E  A  C  H  E
K  E  E  N  S  L  E  E  V  E
D  E  L  E  T  E  S  E  E  N
```

2 Write the words you found in the puzzle beside their definitions.

Across

a. A plan _____

b. A sportsperson _____

c. To instruct _____

d. Players on the same side in a game _____

e. To touch _____

f. A thing with moving parts which needs some kind of power to do its job _____

g. A chair _____

h. A deep, narrow valley _____

i. Every _____

j. Enthusiastic _____

k. An arm of a coat _____

l. To cross out _____

m. Past participle of see _____

Down

a. The opposite of *sour* _____

b. An office restaurant _____

c. High temperature _____

d. What we do with food _____

e. Connected with the sea _____

f. The back of the shoe _____

g. December 31 is New Year's _____

h. To take without asking _____

i. A thing which happens while you're asleep _____

j. The wife of a king _____

3   Complete the words in the text below by writing **ie** or **ei**. The first one has been done for you.

Please write a br____f p____ce about the rel____f work in the Sudan. We bel____ve the

work you did in this f____ld was for charity organisations who rec____ve medicines from the

West and teach hyg____ne. We do not wish to dec____ve the public who often

perc____ve the problem in Africa as ch____fly one of lack of food, particularly prot____n.

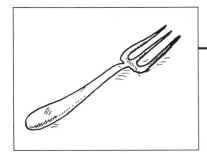

2

/ɔː/

The sound /ɔː/ can be spelt in many different ways. The easiest to remember are:

or   (*eg*: born fort)
ore (*eg*: core shore)

But /ɔː/ can also be spelt:

ar (*eg*: war)	**augh** (*eg*: caught)	**oor** (*eg*: door)	**aw** (*eg*: law)
our (*eg*: four)	**ough** (*eg*: fought)	**al** (*eg*: walk)	**au** (*eg*: author)

PRACTICE

1   Complete this poem using the words in the box.

pause   jaws   paws   thought   claws

Their feet are called _____

Their nails are called _____

They open their _____

And eat without _____

For _____

2 Match the words on the left with the definition on the right.

a.	astronaut	1	opposite of *peace*
b.	board	2	past tense of *catch*
c.	brought	3	past tense of *see*
d.	call	4	you eat with this
e.	caught	5	a person who goes into space
f.	chalk	6	it belongs to you
g.	fork	7	past tense of *bring*
h.	more	8	teachers write on it
i.	poor	9	opposite of *rich*
j.	yours	10	to telephone
k.	war	11	opposite of *less*
l.	saw	12	you write on a blackboard with this

3 Find the mystery word by filling in the missing letters. All the words contain the sound /ɔː/ .

Clues

a. where patients sleep in a hospital

b. past tense of *teach*

c. system of rules

d. meat from a pig

e. not believable

f. the place where you play golf

g. past tense of *buy*

h. you use this in the sea

i. under the ceiling

j. another word for *speak*

k. to put in

l. not interested

Mystery word:

3

/uː/

The sound /uː/ can be written in several different ways. It is often spelt with a **u**:

u (*eg*: tuna super)
u + consonant + **e** (*eg*: rule June)
ue (*eg*: blue true)
ui (*eg*: fruit suit)

It can also be spelt:

ew (*eg*: flew chew)
oe (*eg*: shoe canoe)

> *But be careful!*
> In many of these words /uː/ is preceded by /j/ (*eg*: use rescue new).

Other common ways of spelling /uː/ use the letter **o**:

o (*eg*: who do)
oo (*eg*: spoon boot)
o + consonant + **e** (*eg*: move whose)
ou (*eg*: route soup)

PRACTICE

I Find all the words with the sound /uː/ in this puzzle.

```
V  A  L  U  E  K  P  U  R  S  U  E  P  I  O
I  X  O  G  U  S  U  A  L  W  E  R  H  S  X
E  I  O  H  A  B  O  O  T  R  H  C  U  S  C
W  N  S  U  I  T  C  A  S  E  P  H  M  U  O
W  T  E  H  T  O  A  R  S  U  S  E  O  E  M
L  O  N  E  W  S  A  G  E  N  T  W  U  K  P
H  U  G  E  S  H  V  U  M  I  U  T  R  Z  U
A  W  N  Y  H  O  D  E  B  T  P  E  W  S  T
C  H  O  O  S  E  W  R  T  E  I  K  A  P  E
H  G  O  M  F  L  B  P  R  O  D  U  C  E  R
W  E  N  R  Z  O  O  C  O  F  F  D  U  T  Y
O  P  P  O  R  T  U  N  I  T  Y  L  I  P  D
```

2   Write the words you found in the puzzle beside their definitions.

Across
a. When someone like a policeman or a nurse is not needed at work
(2 words) _____ _____

b. You put your clothes in this when you go on holiday _____

c. What something is worth to you _____

d. A chance to do something _____

e. To run after or chase something _____

f. Normal or customary _____

g. A seat that people sit on in a church _____

h. Footwear that covers the leg _____

i. A place to go and see animals in cages _____

j. A person who arranges the making of a TV programme or film _____

k. To employ something for a purpose (eg: I . . . a toothbrush to clean my teeth.) _____

l. A person who owns a shop from where you can buy papers, tobacco etc _____

m. To pick or select something _____

n. Very large, enormous _____

Down
a. Opposite of *clever* or *sensible* _____

b. A very fast electronic machine for typing letters or doing calculations _____

c. 12 o'clock midday _____

d. A number of printed copies produced at the same time (eg: newspapers) _____

e. Opposite of *out of* _____

f. What you can see through the window _____

g. To break up food in your mouth _____

h. Footwear that covers the foot _____

i. The ability to find something funny _____

j. Opposite of *to tighten* _____

k. To disagree or debate about something _____

l. To bring together as one _____

4

/ʌ/

The sound /ʌ/ is usually spelt:

u (*eg*: must shut butter hut)
o (*eg*: love mother cover)
ough (*eg*: rough tough)

PRACTICE

Complete the poem by using the words in the box. All the words have the sound /ʌ/.

sunny	come	worry	honey	tonne	some	son	hurry	curry	love
money	glove	none	dove						

1 Bees make _____

2 Workers make _____

3 The weather can be _____
   And jokes can be funny.

4 Indians make _____

5 Exams make you _____

6 Clocks make you _____
   Alarms make you scurry.

7 1 minus 1 makes _____

8 A thousand kilos make a _____

9 A baby boy – your little _____
   Congratulations! Well done.

10 A lovely white bird's called a _____

11 A couple holding hands call it _____

12 A quiet night in is all right for _____

13 But here's a party invitation for those who want to _____

Common words which include the sound /ʌ/

above	courage	month	oven	tongue
accompany	discover	mother	recover	tonne
among	done	none	rough	tough
another	enough	nothing	shovel	trouble
become	glove	once	some	welcome
brother	love	one	sometimes	won
come	Monday	other	son	young
couple				

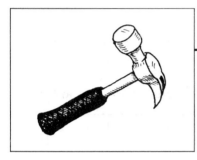

5
/ə/

The sound /ə/ is very common in English and is spelt in many different ways. However, as a vowel sound on its own, it is *never* found in stressed syllables (*eg*: **bet**ter /ˈbetə/, **amuse** /əˈmjuːz/, **Saturday** /ˈsætədeɪ/.

PRACTICE

1 Underline the syllables which contain the sound /ə/ in the words below. List the ways you found to spell /ə/.

afraid	data	tonight
sugar	father	mirror
statement	important	centre
employment	nation	dignity
human	status	helpfully
figure		

2 Complete the words in these sentences by spelling the sound /ə/.

__ hundr__d ph__togr__ph__ __s fr__m Can__d__ __nd __meric__ __rrived in

Britain t__ join th__ discuss__ __n in Lond__n __bout th__ role __f television __nd

newspap__ __s when r__porting fr__m war zones. There has so far been no __greement

with governm__nts on __bolishing vis__ c__ntrol or on pr__viding signific__nt

improvem__nts in consul__ __ __ssist__nce __broad.

6

/ɪə/

The sound /ɪə/ can be spelt in a number of ways:

ear   (*eg*: fear rear)
eer   (*eg*: beer cheer)
ere   (*eg*: here severe)
ier   (*eg*: frontier pier)

PRACTICE

Complete the letter below using the words in the box.

we're   nearer   interfere   cashiers   severe   clear   dear   volunteers
sincerely   engineer   appears   year

_____ Members of Staff

It _____ that as the end of the _____ comes _____ we will need some

_____ to help the _____ at the check-out. I hope this will not _____

with your holiday plans.

Also, according to the _____, it is _____ that the damage to the machines is

due to the _____ temperatures _____ having at the moment, so please

cover your machines when you leave the office.

Yours _____

J D De Vere

7

/eɪ/

The sound /eɪ/ can be spelt in several different ways. It is nearly always spelt with an **a**:

a (*eg*: able station)
a + consonant + **e** or **y** (*eg*: face lazy)
a + **nge** (*eg*: dangerous strange)
ay (*eg*: stay payment)
ai (*eg*: aim remain)

> *But be careful!*
> There are exceptions. Words spelt **are, air** or **any** (*eg*: fare fair many) are not usually pronounced /eɪ/.

It can also be spelt:

ei (*eg*: weight freight)

It is also found in the following words:

great break steak they

PRACTICE

Unscramble the words to finish the letter. All the words contain the sound /eɪ/.

Dear (naJe)

How was your (oyilhad) in the (satSte)? It's a nice (alcpe) to have a (kaber), isn't it? I hope you weren't too (aridfa). So many people (ysa) New York is a (zaycr) city but I couldn't (coplmina) about my own (tsay) in the USA. I felt quite (fase).

I went on an (chaexnge) visit with a friend at school who was the (mase) (gea). His father was a (repiant) called (aviDd) (aCpe). I remember that his favourite meal was (taeks) and chips.

What was the weather like? When I was there we had a lot of (niar). Especially the (yad) we went to a (mage) of (sabellab). They had to stop it. I didn't mind as no-one could (xeplina) it to me (nyawya)!

Must go now. I've got a (rinat) to catch. I (amy) have a new job in TV. I'm still in search of (mafe)!

Lots of love

(orraLine)

8

/aɪ/

The sound /aɪ / can be spelt in several different ways. It is nearly always spelt with an **i**:

i   (*eg*: find mild quiet)
i + consonant + **e** or **y**   (*eg*: quite tiny)
igh   (*eg*: sigh light)

It can also be spelt with a **y**:

y   (*eg*: my fly cycle)

PRACTICE

Unscramble the letters and match the words in the box to the definitions or clues. All the words contain the sound /aɪ /.

| gtlih oplit ebdir ginht-meit sticcly ybu sseid sirhl cibelcy tnhin |
| ekils semicr hys iel nibdl tangi demiblc fekin Fayrid lichd |

1 A two-wheeled vehicle

2 Someone who rides number 1

3 Someone who cannot see is _____

4 Jo _____ summer because it's usually nice and warm.

5 Turn on the _____. It's dark in here.

6 He was so tall that we called him a _____!

7 Have you ever _____ a mountain?

8 A person who flies an aircraft is a _____

9 A woman on her wedding day is a _____

10 I've got a _____ but I haven't got a fork.

11 Monday, Tuesday, Wednesday, Thursday, _____

12 In the daytime it's light but in the _____ _____ it's dark.

13 I'm going to the shop to _____ some food.

14 A triangle has three _____

15 Fifth, sixth, seventh, eighth, _____

16 Someone from Ireland is _____

17 Murder, theft and burglary are all _____

18 He's very _____ and doesn't like meeting new people.

19 Don't _____ in bed. Get up and have breakfast.

20 I knew her when she was a little _____ of nine.

9

/əʊ/

The sound /əʊ/ can be spelt in **several different ways. The most common** are:

oa (*eg*: coat road)
ow (*eg*: glow flow)
o + consonant + **e** (*eg*: vote nose)
o + consonant + **y** (*eg*: rosy cosy)

PRACTICE

Complete the crossword. All the words contain the sound /əʊ/.

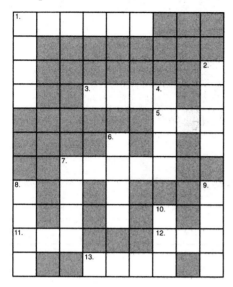

Across

1 Opposite of *adore*

3 If you haven't got enough money to buy the car, you need to ask the bank for a
_____

5 The seeds of this tree are called acorns.

7 A piece of rock

11 A word for *cut the grass*

12 I'm quite independent – I enjoy travelling on my _____

13 In summer, the winds _____ from the south-east.

Down

1 Bread is shaped into a _____ for baking.

2 Yesterday I _____ up at 6 am but I didn't get up until 8 am.

4 A word for *a short letter*

6 The male of this animal has horns and a little beard.

7 I'd like to see your holiday photos – can you _____ them to me?

8 The place where you live

9 He spoke in a very angry _____ of voice.

12 Opposite of *high*

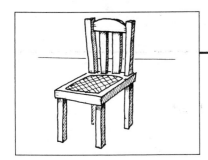

/eə/

The sound /eə/ can be spelt in a number of ways:

are (*eg*: software care)
air (*eg*: chair hair)
ear (*eg*: bear wear)
ere (*eg*: there where)

The following words also contain the sound /eə/

million**aire** m**ayor** th**eir**

PRACTICE

Complete the crossword. All the words contain the sound /eə/.

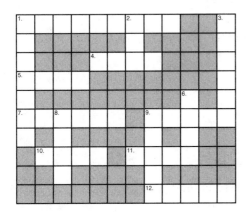

Across

1 A bad dream
4 Money paid for a journey
5 It covers your head.
7 Mend or fix
9 _____ is she? She's over there.
10 Many people from Sweden have
_____ hair.
11 I bought a _____ of shoes.
12 There's only one, so we must
_____ it.

Down

1 Opposite of *everywhere*
2 We need to breathe this all the time.
3 A shape with four equal sides
6 Open it carefully, don't _____
the paper.
8 A fruit
9 He usually _____ a tie to work.

11

/ʃ/

The sound /ʃ/ is spelt in various ways. The easiest to remember is:

sh (*eg*: sheep ship fashion fresh)

Sometimes it is spelt:

ch (*eg*: chef chalet chaperon)

The sound /ʃ/ can also be spelt with:

t (*eg*: section Egyptian initial cautious)
c (*eg*: electrician commercial efficient delicious ocean)
s (*eg*: extension pension suspension)
ss (*eg*: profession session confession)
x (*eg*: anxious)

Occasionally the sound /ʃ/ at the beginning of a word is spelt:

s (*eg*: sugar sure)

PRACTICE

Underline the letters which are pronounced /ʃ/ in the following texts.

1 If you are anxious about future generations, please give a generous donation to our organisation. We have a special social and educational programme. We also have irrigation and conservation projects, and a programme of vaccination against infectious disease. We need your financial support. We are sure that you will help us take action.

2 There was a lot of shouting at immigration because one of the musicians did not show her identification. The official did not believe her explanation and refused her permission to enter the station.

3 The ambitious language learner, who wants to do some translation after graduation, should work hard on pronunciation and dictation as well as conversation.

4 The exhibition which opens tomorrow reflects the passion of one man. After years of exploration into this ancient civilisation, Dr Ignatious brings us his impressions of Grecian life.

12 /f/

The sound /f/ is normally spelt:

f   (*eg*: fall toffee fence cafeteria)

However, many English words which come from ancient Greek words spell /f/:

ph   (*eg*: philharmonic phial epigraph)

PRACTICE

1   Look at these ancient Greek words and their definitions. Use these definitions to help you work out the meanings of the words in the box below. Check with a dictionary if you are not sure.

> phonemes   anglophile   telegraph   telephone   physical science
>
> arachnophobia   philosophy   philanthropist   photography   pharmacist

photos = light	philos = loving	pharmakon = medicine
sophos = wise	phobia = fear/hatred	tele = far away
arachne = spider	physis = nature	graphos = writing or recording
phone = sound/voice	anthropos = man	

2   Match the words in the box above with the definition below.

a. A person who wants to help mankind _____

b. A person who prepares and sells drugs _____

c. A logical study of thought, knowledge, the universe _____

d. The process of making pictures using light _____

e. A person who loves English things _____

f. An instrument which sends voices over long distances _____

g. A system for sending messages over long distances _____

h. The individual sounds of a language _____

i. A fear of spiders _____

j. The study of natural forces such as gravity and energy _____

13

Final c or ic

Most adjectives and nouns that end in **c** (or **ic**) have a regular spelling even when they change into adverbs or adjectives; for example:

dramatic – dramatically   republic – republican
athletic – athletically   statistic – statistical

(For more detailed rules about the adverb ending, see the later section 'Adding **ly** to form adverbs'.)

However, there is a small group of words ending in **c** that add **k** when forming participles and past tenses or nouns:

panic – panicking/panicked/panicker
picnic – picnicking/picnicked/picnicker
mimic – mimicking/mimicked
traffic – trafficking/trafficked/trafficker

PRACTICE

Fill in the missing **k** if it is needed. Use the parts of speech of the word to help you.

1 My mother insisted I had a music___al education.

2 Don't be such a panic___er! We'll sort out the problem.

3 The school inspector was very critic___al of the lessons she had seen.

4 If it's a nice day we'll go picnic___ing in the woods.

5 My father was an electric___al engineer.

6 This problem is basic___ally very simple to solve.

7 This new coffee maker is mechanic___ally very simple.

8 I love the supermarket doors that open automatic___ally.

9 The customs officer opened the case and found the heroin that the drugs traffic___er had hidden in the bottom.

10 She researched the problem systematic___ally from beginning to end.

11 Jo was very popular with the other kids because she was always mimic___ing the teachers.

14

Final /k/

The sound /k/ at the end of a word is spelt differently depending upon what sound comes before it.

After a consonant, a dipthong or a long vowel sound, /k/ is usually spelt with a **k**:

k   (*eg*: milk thank break)
ke   (*eg*: smoke coke)

There is one common exception: ache

After a short vowel, /k/ is usually spelt **c** or **ck**:

c   (*eg*: music terrific Zodiac)
ck   (*eg*: black pick check)

There are five common exceptions: hook look took book cook

There is also a small group of words that are spelt:
que   (*eg*: cheque technique unique)

PRACTICE

Choose the correct spelling.

1 Why don't we go for a walk/walck in the park/parck?
2 If you've got a headake/headache, take an aspirin.
3 You can't wear red soks/socks with those shoes!
4 Have you put out the knives and forks/forcks?
5 Have you got an elastic/elastik band I can tie up my hair with?
6 The answers are at the bak/back of the book/boock.
7 I'm going to bake/bache a cake/cacke this afternoon.
8 He's off work/worck because he's feeling sik/sick.
9 Good luk/luck with the new job.
10 He has a basic/basick understanding of the subject.
11 He didn't make/mache any mistakes/mistaches.
12 Let's go for a drink/drinck in the pub.
13 What do you think/thinck of my new mountain bike/biche?
14 The giraffe has the longest nek/neck of all the animals.
15 My American cousin always says *truk/truck* instead of *lorry*.
16 I went to an interesting talk/talck on modern art last night.
17 Have you heard the joke/joche about the mouse and the elephant?

18 My dog never fetches the stiks/sticks we throw to him.
19 That's a unic/unique painting on your wall.
20 This is a historic/historick occasion for our countries.

15

Final /tʃ/

The sound /tʃ/ at the end of a word is spelt differently depending upon what sound comes before it.

After a consonant, a dipthong or a long vowel sound, /tʃ/ is usually spelt:

ch   (*eg*: arch lunch coach couch speech beach)

After a short vowel, /tʃ/ is usually spelt:

tch   (*eg*: catch fetch pitch)

> ***But be careful!***
> There are five common words where /tʃ/ follows a short vowel and is spelt **ch**:
>   much such rich which attach

PRACTICE

Choose the correct spelling.

1 The football pich/pitch is near the church/churtch.
2 She used a torch/tortch to light up the darkened cellar.
3 The coach/coatch reached/reatched the station on time.
4 I've just bought a Swiss wach/watch.
5 The beach/beatch at Brighton is polluted.
6 The customer asked the waiter to fech/fetch a mach/match for his cigar.
7 Can you touch/toutch the branch/brantch of that tree?
8 The pach/patch of grass near the dich/ditch is very wet and muddy.
9 The Pope has preached/preatched in every continent of the world.
10 Take this bunch/buntch of flowers to Mrs Finch/Fintch.

16

Adding endings to final y

When a word ends in a consonant + **y**, the final **y** changes to **i**; for example:

carry – carried
funny – funnier
happy – happily
certify – certifiable

The final **y** changes to **ie** when adding **s**; for example:

hurry – hurries
curry – curries
story – stories

When a word ends in a vowel + **y**, the **y** remains when adding an ending; for example:

pray – prays
way – ways
donkey – donkeys
storey – storeys

When you add **ing** to any word ending in **y**, the **y** remains; for example:

fly – flying   enjoy – enjoying

PRACTICE

Complete the crossword using the clues below.

Across

1 Large buildings where things are made

3 His mother _____ about him when he goes parachuting.

5 Real or imaginary events told to you

8 Things that are not true

9 People who try to discover another country's secrets

11 Animals with long ears, often thought to be lazy

13 Light from the sun comes in _____

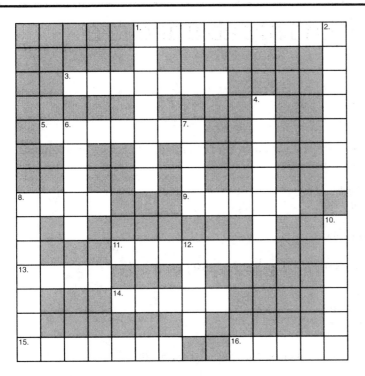

14 Joe is musical and _____ the guitar and the piano.

15 Another word for *the floors of a building*

16 Insects that carry a lot of diseases

Down

1 Ships that carry people and cars across the sea

2 My sister _____ at Sussex University.

4 Tree-climbing animals with long tails that look similar to us

6 He _____ on a different hat every week but he never buys anything.

7 That woman always _____ 'Good morning' to us.

8 Large vehicles that carry many things around the country

10 He loves being with children, so he _____ helping at the local school.

12 Needed to open your locked doors.

Endings able and ible

The suffix **able** is added to certain nouns and verbs to make adjectives. It is usually added to *complete* words; for example:

enjoy	–	enjoyable
comfort	–	comfortable
count	–	countable
reason	–	reasonable

Most verbs ending in **e** drop the **e** before adding **able**; for example:

like	–	likable
believe	–	believable
forgive	–	forgivable

However, when **e** follows **c** or **g**, it is not dropped; for example:

notice	–	noticeable
replace	–	replaceable
change	–	changeable
knowledge	–	knowledgeable
manage	–	manageable

The suffix **ible** is less common.
It is usually added to *part* of a word to make an adjective. The suffix **ible** often follows:

ss or **s**

possible	accessible
responsible	sensible
visible	reversible

Exceptions: disposable   indispensable   excuseable

rr

horrible   terrible

ince and **ge**

convincible	invincible
intelligible	illegible

Note: the final **e** is dropped from the stem

pt and **st**

corruptible   perceptible
digestible   resistible

Exceptions: acceptable   adjustable   detestable

Other common words spelt **ible**:

edible   incredible   audible   flexible   infallible   compatible

As there are many more words which end **able** than **ible**, if you are not sure it is probably advisable to add **able**.

PRACTICE

Complete the words in the sentences below by adding **able** or **ible**. Make any spelling changes that are needed.

1 I think higher taxes are prefer_____ to higher unemployment.

2 The company has been profit_____ since it started.

3 She is a friendly and person_____ young woman.

4 The UN report says the conditions in Sudan are terr_____

5 Of course the water is drink_____

6 I don't think the work is manage_____ for one person alone.

7 Is your room comfort_____?

8 His story was full of lies and completely unbeliev_____

9 It is now poss_____ to fly to the USA in under 5 hours.

10 This video is only us_____ in America and Japan.

11 His cooking was so bad that the food was indigest_____

12 Is it accept_____ to wear jeans to the interview?

18

Endings ise and ize

In many multi-syllable words the sounds /aɪz/ can be spelt either **ise** or **ize** as both forms are correct; for example:

realise/realize
recognise/recognize
civilise/civilize
apologise/apologize
sympathise/sympathize
criticise/criticize

It is common in British spelling to choose **ise** and in American spelling to choose **ize**. It is important to be consistent in your spelling. You should decide whether to use **ise** or **ize** and then spell all words this way.

> *But be careful!*
> Some single-syllable words can only be spelt **ize**. The most common examples are:
>   prize   size
>
> Other words can only be spelt **ise**. The most common examples are:
>   rise   surprise
>   wise   advertise
>   advise   televise
>   exercise

PRACTICE

Fill in the missing letters (**s** or **z**) in the sentences below. Some words can be spelt both ways. Decide which spelling you prefer and use this for all the words where you have a choice.

1 Louise won a pri__e at school for her painting.

2 I apologi__e for phoning at such a late hour.

3 The government wants to stop tobacco adverti__ing on TV.

4 The doctor advi__ed her to take more exerci__e.

5 I sympathi__e with any parents of young children during the summer holiday.

6 It was such a lovely surpri__e to see my brother again.

7 I wish you would stop critici___ing my driving!

8 What si___e is that dress? It looks lovely.

9 I think you are wi___e to think about life insurance.

10 I never reali___ed you knew Simon too.

Some common words which are *only* spelt -ise

advertise   clockwise   compromise   despise   disguise
enterprise   exercise   franchise   improvise   otherwise
merchandise   revise   rise   sunrise   televise

19

Endings s and es

Normally both plural nouns and third person singular verbs are formed by adding **s**:

s   baths   books
He makes model aeroplanes.

But words ending in **ch, sh, x** and **s** add **es**:

ch	beaches	My wife teaches young children.
sh	dishes	She finishes work at 5.30.
x	boxes	She relaxes in the swimming pool.
s	buses	The river crosses the frontier.

Words ending in a consonant followed by **y** change **y** to **i** and add **es**:

babies   ferries   tries
She flies to Paris once a week.
My baby never cries at night.

Words ending in a vowel followed by **y** simply add **s**:

monkeys   stays   enjoys

PRACTICE

I Change the word in brackets into the correct plural or third person form.

    a. Mary (watch_____) a lot of foreign television.

    b. She (find_____) it interesting.

    c. It (help_____) her to practise her language.

    d. Mary (think_____) that Paris is expensive.

    e. But most (city_____) are expensive nowadays.

    f. Many have high local (tax_____).

    g. Many (company_____) are moving out to cheaper towns.

    h. However, they cannot keep their trained (worker_____).

    i. My son (miss_____) living in London.

    j. He (say_____) the country is boring.

    k. He (wish_____) he had stayed in the city.

    l. He cannot get the (book_____) for his (study_____).

2 Here is a page from a student's homework book. There are ten words that are wrongly spelt. Find them and correct them.

> My brother David lives in Sydney where he workes for a Japanese computer company. They make office machines such as typewriteres and word processors. He deals with the workers' pay conditions.
>
> His wife Sandy is a nurse who helps old people. Sometimes she visites them in their homes and sometimes she takes them to the hospital. Their daughter Zoe is seven yeares old. She goes to school every day but when she comes home she likes playing with the dog and cat. After she finishs her homework she usually watches TV.
>
> On Sundays my brother playes hockey. Sometimes Sandy, Zoe and the dog go to watch one of his matchs. Afterwards David drives to one of the beachs nearby. Everybody swims except for the dog who runs along the sand and barkes at the waves. Sometimes Zoe thinks she is a dog too and copys him until my brother gets angry and shouts at them both to stop.

Irregular plurals

To make the plural of some nouns ending in a single **f** or **fe**, the ending is replaced by **ves**; for example:

half – halves
life – lives

Some nouns do not take **s** at all, but make vowel changes to form the plural. For example:

man   – men
woman – women

Most nouns ending in **o** simply add **s**. Others, however, add **es**.

PRACTICE

1   Match the words to the pictures.

> a. knives   b. wives   c. shelves   d. loaves   e. thieves   f. leaves   g. calves

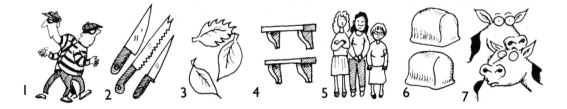

2   Complete the words using the vowels in the box below.

> ee   i   oo   ou

a.   You clean your t_____th with a t_____thbrush.

b.   One m_____se in a house is all right.
    Three m_____ce are not so nice.

c.   Twelve inches equals one f_____t
    Three f_____t equals one yard.

3   Find the mistakes. Which three words in the list below should be spelt **es**?

a. radios   b. videos   c. solos   d. cameos   e. potatos

f. pianos   g. tomatos   h. portfolios   i. heros

4   Now label the pictures correctly.

a. _____   b. _____   c. _____   d. _____   e. _____

f. _____   g. _____   h. _____   i. _____

21

Adding suffixes to words ending in e

To decide whether to drop the final **e** when adding a suffix, first look at the second to last letter.

Is it a consonant?
Is it **c** or **g**?
Is it a vowel?

consonant + e	ce or ge	vowel + e	ee
type	notice	value	free
write	face	argue	agree
come	encourage	tiptoe	disagree
telephone	change		

Now look at these tables which set out the rules for adding suffixes to words ending in **e**:

Consonant + e		Examples
Suffix beginning with a vowel (eg: **ing, ed**)	Drop the final **e**.	time – timing
Suffix beginning with a consonant (eg: **ment, less, ful**)	Keep the final **e**.	time – timeless

ce or ge		Examples
Suffix beginning with a vowel	Drop the final **e** before **ing** and **ed**.	notice – noticing
	Keep the final **e** before suffixes beginning **o, a** or **u**.	notice – noticeable
Suffix beginning with a consonant	Keep the final **e**.	encourage – encouragement

Vowel + e		Examples
Suffix beginning with a vowel	Drop the final **e**.	argue – arguing
Suffix beginning with a consonant	Drop the final **e**.	argue – argument

To add the suffix **ing** to a word ending in **ie**, we change the **i** to **y**; for example:

die – dying
lie – lying

When adding a suffix to words ending in **ee**, keep the final **e**, except before **ed**.

disagree disagreement disagreed

But be careful!
There are some exceptions:
    mile   – mileage   nine – ninth
    whole – wholly   awe – awful

PRACTICE

I Look at the four lists of words at the beginning of this section. Make new words from these by adding suffixes to them. Choose suffixes that fit from this list:

ation   er   ly
ing   ment ist
ed   ful
able   less

2 Read the letter below. There are seven mistakes among the underlined words. Find the mistakes and correct them.

I am <u>writeing</u> to thank you for <u>haveing</u> us to stay and to let you know that the <u>improvments</u> on our house have now been <u>completed</u> and <u>hopefully</u> we can move in very soon. We are <u>driving</u> there next Saturday. The children are <u>extremly</u> excited about <u>living</u> in such a beautiful house, but I'm a little worried about keeping the <u>valueable</u> furniture <u>safely</u> away from them!

<u>Hoping</u> you'll be <u>comeing</u> to visit us soon.

Yours <u>truely</u>

3 Choose the correct suffix and write the word out in full.

a. The weather in Britain is very _____ (change – **able/ous**)

b. Only very _____ people leave their umbrellas at home (courage – **ing/ous**)

c. Everyone looks forward to _____ the sun. (see – **ed/ing**)

d. However, there is _____ among the experts about how good the sun is for you. (disagree – **ment/ly**)

e. Some _____ people say the sun is good for your health. (knowledge – **able/ful**)

f. Others say it speeds up the _____ process. (age – **ous/ing**)

g. I am still _____ who to believe. (decide – **ed/ing**)

h. It is _____ that they are both right. (like – **less/ly**)

i. Their _____ just support their own theories. (calculate – **ations/ments**)

Adding suffixes to one-syllable words ending in a consonant

If a one-syllable word ends in one vowel + one consonant, the final consonant is doubled before suffixes **ed, er, est, ing** and **y**. For example:

swim – swimming – swimmer
fun – funny
can – canned – canning
cat – catty

> **Rule**
> - one syllable
> - one vowel
> - one consonant – double it!

The exceptions are the consonants **w, y** and **x**; for example:

bow – bowed
box – boxing
play – player

If a one-syllable word ends in two consonants, or two vowels + one consonant, the final consonant is not doubled. For example:

seem – seemed – seeming
catch – catching – catcher
cheap – cheaper – cheapest

PRACTICE

I   Which of these words double the final consonant? Write in the consonant where necessary.

Examples

I remember shut _t_ ing the door.

He was shout___ing at me.

a. It's wet___er here than at home.

b. I hate wait___ing for the bus in the rain.

c. Weed___ing the garden is a tiring job.

d. They had their wed___ing in the local church.

e. It must be the hot___est day of the year.

f. The driver hoot___ed at the dog crossing the road.

g. You can't see her now, she's sleep___ing.

h. I enjoy shop___ing in London.

i. This cake will make me even fat___er.

j. If you want to go on a diet, you must buy a book on slim___ing.

k. You look thin___er than when I last saw you.

23

Adding suffixes to multi-syllable words ending in a consonant

When the last syllable is stressed and it ends in one vowel + one consonant, double the final consonant. For example:

    begin   – beginning
    commit   – committed
    recap   – recapping

When the last syllable is not stressed, do not double the final consonant. For example:

    reckon   – reckoned
    reason   – reasoned
    happen   – happening

When the last syllable contains two vowels, do not double the final consonant. For example:

    conceal – concealed
    mention – mentioning

But be careful!
Look at the next section on words ending in l (*eg*: tràvel – tràvelled).

Certain compound words do not follow these rules (*eg*: typewritten
gravedigger outrigger).

PRACTICE

1   Which of these words double the final consonant? Write in the consonant where
necessary.

a.   It occùr___ed to me that what màtter___ed most was the devèlop___ment of new
opportunities.

b.   I regrèt ___ed having pròfit___ed from the mistakes of other people and bènefit___ed from
their downfall.

c.   In my speech of resignation I refèr___ed to what I called an unjust law which permìt___ed
such activities.

d.   I prefèr___ed to leave.

2   Match the words on the right with the definitions on the left and double the final
consonant where necessary.

1 money you receive after a relative dies	a. an ìron___ing board
2 a large room where groups of people eat	b. the màrket___ing department
3 an elderly person who no longer works	c. defèr___ed payment
4 the section in a company which deals with advertising	d. a pènsion___er
5 payment made at a later date	e. a transmìt___er
6 where clothes are pressed	f. a bànquet___ing hall
7 how to lose weight	g. lìmit___ed edition
8 a small number of books published	h. inhèrit___ed wealth
	i. a dìet___ing programme

24

Adding suffixes to words ending in l

When adding **ed, ing, er, ent,** or **ation** to a word ending in l, follow these rules.

Double the final l when it comes after a single vowel; for example:

travel – travelled – traveller – travelling
model – modelled – modeller – modelling
shovel – shovelled – shoveller – shovelling

Do not double the final l when it comes after two vowels; for example:

trail – trailed – trailer – trailing
boil – boiled – boiler – boiling

> **But be careful!**
> If l comes after **ue**, double the l (*eg*: fuel – fuelled   duel – duelled
> gruel – gruelling).

PRACTICE

1 Complete the words in each sentence by adding the correct ending.

Example
They travel__*led*__ to Istanbul by train.

  a. Jackson's time in the race equal_____ the world record.

  b. Pick up the folder label_____ with your name.

  c. Martin heard the sound of the propel_____ as the old plane started up.

  d. The bomb exploded in the shopping centre and fatal_____ injured five people.

  e. We regret to announce the cancel_____ of the 8.05 train to Brighton due to technical difficulties.

2 Complete the words in these sentences. Be careful – not all the words double the final l.

  a. I've boil_____ some water for coffee. Do you want a cup?

  b. The neighbours often heard them quarrel_____ about money.

c. Three policemen were kill_____ in the accident.

d. You fail_____ your exams because you didn't work hard enough.

e. I'm not feel_____ very well so I'm staying at home today.

f. The wine was excel_____.

g. Talk to an employment counsel_____ about finding a new job.

h. The lighting is control_____ by this button here.

25

Adding ly to form adverbs

Adverbs are normally formed by adding **ly** to an adjective; for example:

light	– lightly
brave	– bravely
cruel	– cruelly
natural	– naturally
definite	– definitely
special	– specially

However, if the adjective ends in **y** then the **y** is changed to **i** before adding **ly**; for example:

funny	– funnily
happy	– happily
military	– militarily

If the adjective ends in **le** then the **e** is dropped and only **y** is added; for example:

simple	– simply
possible	– possibly
probable	– probably
humble	– humbly

If the adjective ends in **ic** then **ally** is added; for example:

automatic	– automatically
geographic	– geographically
photographic	– photographically

> *But be careful!*
> There are exceptions. Here are some of the common ones:
>
> true – truly   public – publicly
> shy – shyly   whole – wholly
> sly – slyly

Not all adverbs are formed by adding **ly** to adjectives. Some adverbs have the same form as adjectives (*eg*: early fast).
Some adjectives change form completely (*eg*: good – well).

PRACTICE

1   Complete the sentences below with the correct form of the adverb.

a. Anne answered all the questions _____. (correct)

b. The cinema is _____ full. (complete)

c. We can eat _____ in this restaurant. (inexpensive)

d. Frank looked at her _____. (unhappy)

e. The magician was _____ assisted by his young son. (able)

f. The windows in my mother's car are _____ operated. (electric)

g. Their house was _____ decorated. (attractive)

h. My son has been _____ accused of murder. (false)

i. Repairs are _____ done by the mechanic. (normal)

j. Put that down and come over here _____. (immediate)

2   Complete the story by writing adverbs in the blanks. Choose any word you like from the appropriate lists below. Don't forget to make the words into adverbs.

The man walked (a) _____ into the cabaret bar. On stage a woman was singing (b) _____. Around the room the waiters and waitresses worked (c) _____. At the table nearest the stage a couple ate (d) _____. He sat down and looked around. The waitress came over and greeted him (e) _____. The man looked at her (f) _____.

(**a**)	(**b**)	(**c**)	(**d**)	(**e**)	(**f**)
quiet	sweet	busy	hungry	polite	kind
calm	loud	careful	quick	rude	angry
lazy	soft	honest	health	warm	sad

26

Homophones

Some words have the same pronunciation but very different spellings. There is no rule for these. They have to be memorised.

brake	break	here	hear	stairs	stares
meet	meat	week	weak	fair	fare
bare	bear	there	their	hair	hare
see	sea	main	mane	sew	so
deer	dear	tail	tale	would	wood
piece	peace	weather	whether	two	too

PRACTICE

I   Correct the spelling mistakes in the letter below. There are 18 mistakes.

> Deer Jim
>
> Hear I am in Alaska. I've been here for too weaks now and I can't bare the thought of going home. You can see our house in the photograph – it's right next to the see. The waves brake on the beach just in front of the windows. When it's stormy, they look like the manes or tales of white horses. The huge would behind the house is full of dear, hares and bears, and you can walk their for miles and not meat anyone. You can really believe old stories of black magic and whiches. The piece in the evening is wonderful – it is so silent. I go up the stares and sew or read for hours and all I can here is the sea.
>
> Would you like to come and stay? The air fair is really not very expensive. Hope to sea you soon.
>
> Love
> Jennifer

Some other common homophones

air	heir	no	know	sell	cell
ate	eight	not	knot	vain	vein
by	buy	or	oar	waist	waste
current	currant	poor	pour	way	weigh
flower	flour	rain	reign	wait	weight
key	quay	right	write	witch	which
new	knew	road	rode		

Part 2: Pronunciation

 | Letters of the alphabet

The letters of the alphabet can be divided into seven sound groups.

PRACTICE

1 Complete the table below by writing the other letters of the alphabet in their sound groups.

1	2	3	4	5	6	7
/eɪ/	/iː/	/e/	/aɪ/	/əʊ/	/uː/	/ɑː/
a	b	f	i	o	q	r

2   We need to know how to pronounce the letters of the alphabet when we are using abbreviations. Match the abbreviations in the box to the definitions below. Use the sound group numbers from the table to help you.

> AD BBC EC B & B VAT USA ITV VSO RSVP PTO NB PhD LSD IOU
>
> GMT HQ UK GB BA CIA

a. Tax paid when you buy something in Britain (212) ⎯⎯⎯⎯

b. A large country between Mexico and Canada (631) ⎯⎯⎯⎯

c. A qualification after three years at university (21) ⎯⎯⎯⎯

d. The American security organisation (241) ⎯⎯⎯⎯

e. The main office or control centre of an organisation (16) ⎯⎯⎯⎯

f. The time in London from which all world times are fixed (232) ⎯⎯⎯⎯

g. A note to show you have borrowed money from someone (456) ⎯⎯⎯⎯

h. England, Scotland and Wales (22) ⎯⎯⎯⎯

i. Another name for h. (61) ⎯⎯⎯⎯

j. A cheap place to stay (2 & 2) ⎯⎯⎯⎯

k. The public television channel in Britain (222) ⎯⎯⎯⎯

l. A commercial television channel in Britain (422) ⎯⎯⎯⎯

m. An organisation that sends people to work in the Third World (235) ⎯⎯⎯⎯

n. Used to describe years since the birth of Jesus (12) ⎯⎯⎯⎯

o. The political union of European countries (22) ⎯⎯⎯⎯

p. A hallucinogenic drug (332) ⎯⎯⎯⎯

q. Used to point out something important in a text (32) ⎯⎯⎯⎯

r. Used to tell you to look at next page (225) ⎯⎯⎯⎯

s. Written at the end of an invitation when a reply is wanted (7322) ⎯⎯⎯⎯

t. An advanced university degree (212) ⎯⎯⎯⎯

2

Initial a

The pronunciation of a word beginning with **a** depends upon whether it is a one-syllable or a multi-syllable word, and on which syllable is stressed.

One-syllable words are most often pronounced:

/æ/   (*eg*: act apt add)

One-syllable words that end in **e** or begin with **ai** are usually pronounced:

/eɪ/   (*eg*: ache ate aim ail)

One-syllable words which begin with **ar** are usually pronounced:

/ɑː/   (*eg*: arm art arc)

> *But be careful!*
> Common exceptions are:
>   ask /ɑː/   aunt /ɑː/   all /ɔː/   axe /æ/   air /eə/

Multi-syllable words that are stressed on the first syllable are usually pronounced in one of the following three ways:

/æ/   (*eg*: animal apple anchor)
/ɑː/   (*eg*: after artist architect
/eɪ/   (*eg*: able acorn)
/ɔ/   (*eg*: always alter awful)

> *But be careful!*
> There are some common exceptions (*eg*: any /e/   area /eə/)

Multi-syllable words that are not stressed on the first syllable are usually pronounced:

/ə/   (*eg*: about alive ago)

Some words are pronounced:

/ɔ/   (*eg*: almost although already also)

PRACTICE

I   Match the words in the box to the groups of definitions.

agree angry announced accent average among actually away
attend airport age afford aspirin accident album adult apart
arrange always affair

Group A
a. Another word for *really*

b. If you add things together and then divide by the number of things you get the _____

c. Something you did not do on purpose

d. How old you are is your _____

e. Something you swallow to ease pain

Group B
a. Another word for *separate from*

b. Jo and Jim _____ their marriage to their friends.

c. An event or happening

d. The place to catch your plane

e. Another word for *to go to* school is to _____ school.

Group C
a. To plan in advance

b. In the middle of

c. Fred's not here. He's _____ in France.

d. All the time

e. To think the same as someone else

Group D
a. A grown man or woman

b. The way people from a particular area pronounce words

c. To have enough money to do something

d. A book used for keeping stamps, photos and so on

e. Feeling upset or displeased about something

2 One word in each group is pronounced differently from the others. Which one is it and how is it pronounced? How are the rest pronounced?

3 Initial e

When a single **e** comes at the beginning of a word, it is commonly pronounced in one of two ways. In most words it is pronounced:

/e/ (*eg*: edge enemy energetic examination)

There are some common exceptions:

English /ɪ/ equal even evening evil /iː/

In words stressed on the second syllable, **e** is pronounced:

/ɪ/ (*eg*: elàstic evènt embàrrass)

There are some common words that can be pronounced with either an /e/ sound or an /iː/ sound.

economic **e**conomy

PRACTICE

I Label the pictures using the words in the box below.

elbow empty engine educate elephant eleven

a. _____

b. _____

c. _____

d. _____

e. _____

f. _____

2   Which five are pronounced /e/?

3   Which one is pronounced /ɪ/?

4   Match the words in the box with the groups of definitions below.

> enter   experiment   expensive   elect   entire   exchange   excite   end
>
> elder   electric   exercise   excellent

Group A
   a. Complete, whole

   b. Go into a space (eg: a room)

   c. Finish, complete

Group B
   a. Older than (eg: an _____ brother)

   b. Choose especially (eg: political office)

   c. If petrol runs out in the world, we may all have to use _____ cars.

Group C
   a. To cause someone to have strong feelings

   b. To give and to receive

   c. Extremely good

Group D
   a. To try out something new

   b. The opposite of *cheap*

   c. To do activities to improve the mind or body

5   One word in each group is pronounced differently from the others. Which one is it and how is it pronounced? How are the rest pronounced?

Initial i

When **i** starts a word, it is usually pronounced:

/ɪ/   (*eg*: if intelligent important)

However, it is pronounced /aɪ/ in the following common words:

ice icy idea ideal identify idle Ireland iron island item

PRACTICE

1 Label the pictures using the words below.

> ice   ink   initials   iron   inn   invitation   inch   island

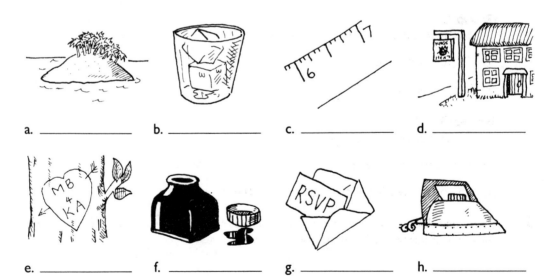

a. _____   b. _____   c. _____   d. _____

e. _____   f. _____   g. _____   h. _____

2 Which five are pronounced /ɪ/?

3 Which three are pronounced /aɪ/?

4 Match the words in the box with the groups of definitions.

> India   immense   imprison   inside   identify   idle   ill   icy   idea

Group A
a. Very large _____

b. Lock up usually as punishment _____

c. A thought or suggestion _____

Group B
a. Lazy _____

b. To recognise or give a name to something _____

c. The opposite of *outside* _____

Group C
a. Coated with frozen water _____

b. Not feeling well _____

c. A large country in Asia _____

5 One word in each group is pronounced differently from the others. Which one is it and how is it pronounced? How are the rest pronounced?

5

Initial o

When **o** starts a word, it is usually pronounced in two ways. In most words it is pronounced:

/ɒ/ (*eg:* obvious off operate)

In words stressed on the second syllable, **o** is pronounced:

/ə/ (*eg:* obey occasion official)

> *But be careful!*
> There are a few common exceptions:
> /əʊ/ (*eg:* only open over own)
> /wʌ/ (*eg:* once one)
> /ʌ/   (*eg:* onion other oven)

(See also the pronunciation of **or** later in this book.)

PRACTICE

1 Match the words in the box with the groups of definitions below.

> observe   obscure   often   opera   obtain   opposition   ox   oxygen   offend
>
> obedient   occupy   occupation

  a. To fill a space (eg: a seat) _____

  b. Happening regularly _____

  c. A musical play _____

  d. To upset someone by what you say or do _____

  e. To watch the actions of others _____

  f. To get or receive something _____

  g. If you do what you are told to do, you are _____

  h. Another word for *your job* _____

  i. Not very common or easy to understand _____

  j. The team you are playing against _____

  k. A large animal used for pulling ploughs and carts _____

2 How is the **o** pronounced in each of these words?

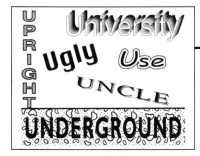

6

Initial u

When **u** starts a word, it is usually pronounced:

/ʌ/   (*eg*: uncle umbrella until unable unimportant)

When the root of the word is *uni*, meaning single, complete or one, **u** is pronounced:

/ju:/ (*eg*: universe United Kingdom unit university)

It is also pronounced /ju:/ when the root of the word is *use*:

/ju:/ (*eg*: usual useful utilise)

PRACTICE

1 Label the pictures below using the words in the box.

> unicycle   uniform   umbrella   upstairs   unicorn   unhappy

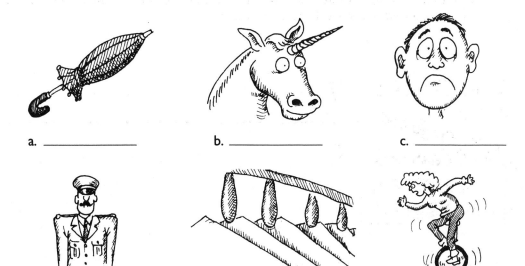

a. _____ b. _____ c. _____

d. _____ e. _____ f. _____

2 Which three are pronounced /ʌ/?

3 Which three are pronounced /ju:/?

4 Match the words in the box with the groups of definitions.

> unable   useless   unisex   upset   unique   uphill   union   uncommon
>
> underline

Group A
a. Not able to be employed for a purpose _____

b. Sad or disappointed _____

c. Movement to the top of a slope _____

Group B

a. A joining together to become one _____

b. The only one of its kind _____

c. If you are _____ to do something, you cannot do it. _____

Group C

a. Rare, not very many _____

b. Emphasise by marking underneath _____

c. Suitable for both men and women _____

5 One word in each group is pronounced differently from the others. Which one is it and how is it pronounced? How are the rest pronounced?

7

C

The letter **c** is pronounced differently depending upon which letter follows it.

Before most consonants and the vowels **a**, **o** and **u**, **c** is pronounced:

/k/ (*eg:* clown crisp cake cover cup)

Before **e, i** or **y, c** is usually pronounced:

/s/ (*eg:* cell circle cycle)

However, if **c** is followed by **ia, ea, iou** or **ien**, it is normally pronounced:

/ʃ/ (*eg:* special ocean precious ancient)

Some common exceptions are:

science scientist scientific

When there are two **cs** together, the first is pronounced /k/ and the second is pronounced /s/:

/ks/ (*eg:* accept succeed)

Some common exceptions:

tobacco accommodation occasion

If **c** is followed by **h**, the two letters normally make one of these three sounds:

/tʃ/ (*eg*: children)
/k/ (*eg*: chemist)
/ʃ/ (*eg*: chauffeur)

(For more detail, see Section 8: **ch**).

PRACTICE

1 /s/, /ʃ/ or /k/? Indicate how the letter **c** is pronounced in these words.

Example
s c ar c e
/k/ /s/

a. su <u>c</u> <u>c</u> ess

b. a <u>c</u> <u>c</u> ept

c. s <u>c</u> ien <u>c</u> e

d. <u>c</u> ymbal

e. <u>c</u> al <u>c</u> ium

f. <u>c</u> urren <u>c</u> y

g. <u>C</u> yprus

h. deli <u>c</u> ious

i. e <u>c</u> <u>c</u> entri <u>c</u>

j. <u>c</u> ro <u>c</u> us

k. appre <u>c</u> iate

l. a <u>c</u> <u>c</u> ess

2 Match the words in the box to the definitions in the groups.

| juice accident twice balcony sufficient car successful decide anchor |
| proficiency accelerate efficient |

Group A
a. Two times _____

b. Liquid from fruit _____

c. To make up your mind _____

Group B
a. A place to stand or sit built outside an upstairs room _____

b. A motor vehicle with four wheels _____

c. A large piece of metal lowered into sea to stop a ship moving _____

Group C

    a. The quality of being good at something _____

    b. Having enough of something _____

    c. Working well _____

Group D

    a. Something you did not want to happen _____

    b. To go faster _____

    c. Getting the result wanted _____

3   How are the **cs** pronounced in each group?

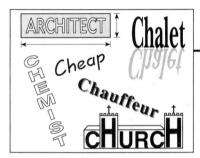

8
ch

The combination **ch** is normally pronounced:

    /tʃ/ (*eg*: church Richard)

In a small group of words it is pronounced:

    /k/ (*eg*: ache anchor architect character chaos chemist Christian psychological scheme school)

Also in a few words **ch** is pronounced:

    /ʃ/ (*eg*: chauffeur chalet chef moustache)

PRACTICE

1   Fill in the spaces with words from the box.

> moustache champion butcher sketch architect chauffeur lunch chefs
>
> kitchen chemist headaches choose

a. The _____ sold Mel 3 kg of rump steak.

b. My house was designed by the best _____ in the city.

c. When I started wearing glasses my _____ stopped.

d. I'm a terrible cook so I never go in the _____.

e. Why did you shave off your _____.

f. My _____ always washes the car on Saturdays.

g. When I'm busy at work I just have a sandwich for _____.

h. I've got to call in at the _____ to buy some toothpaste.

i. When I was young, I was so fast I was the school running _____.

j. It is a very big restaurant – it has two _____.

k. Before she painted the portrait she did a quick _____.

l. I couldn't _____ between the two pairs of shoes.

2   How is the **ch** pronounced in each of these words?

9

ea

The combination **ea** is normally pronounced:

/iː/   (*eg*: eat)

It is also often pronounced:

/e/   (*eg*: head)

> **But be careful!**
> There are some common exceptions (*eg*: create /iːeɪ/   reaction /iːæ/
> break/great /eɪ/   idea/ideal/real /ɪə/

(See also the pronunciation of **ear** in Section 10.)

PRACTICE

1 Find all the words with the letters **ea**. If you do not know how to pronounce any of them, look them up in your dictionary.

```
M  E  A  L  F  B  E  A  C  H
E  X  L  P  E  A  U  W  S  W
A  D  R  E  A  C  H  E  W  E
S  E  E  R  T  H  E  A  E  A
U  A  A  E  H  E  A  L  A  P
R  F  D  A  E  A  V  T  T  O
E  M  Y  D  R  D  Y  H  E  N
C  H  E  A  P  V  O  Y  R  S
S  E  A  S  O  N  B  E  A  K
L  E  A  F  S  T  O  U  T  M
```

2 Write the words you found beside the correct meanings.

a. The first _____ of the day is usually breakfast.

b. He's _____ and can't hear what you are saying.

c. To find out the size of something we must _____ _ it.

d. It is near the sea and often covered in sand.

e. Spring is the _____ which comes after winter.

f. A warm piece of clothing worn on the top half of the body.

g. A gun, a knife or a missile is a kind of _____

h. A small, round, green vegetable

i. Has Anna left _____? Yes, she went ten minutes ago.

j. How _____ are you? I weigh 65 kilos.

k. Can you _____ that book up there? No, I'm not tall enough.

l. The opposite of *expensive*

m. The mouth of a bird

n. A flat, thin, green part of a plant or tree

o. The past tense of *to read*

p. The light, soft covering of a bird's body

q. He never worries about money because his parents are _____

r. The part of the body with the eyes, nose, mouth and ears

s. To make an injury or illness better

ear

The combination **ear** is commonly pronounced in three ways:

/ɪə/ (*eg*: ear dear appear)
/ɜː/ (*eg*: earn early pearl)
/eə/ (*eg*: wear bear swear)

There is one common exception: heart /ɑː/

But be careful!
Don't confuse these two words which look the same but are pronounced differently:
    tear /eə – noun/verb (*eg*: Don't tear the paper. I want to read it.)
    tear /ɪə/ – noun (*eg*: The tears ran down her sad face.)

PRACTICE

1 Match the words in the box to the groups of definitions below.

earnest   years   nearly   rear   earthquake   beard   search   clear   Earth

hear   pear   gears

Group A
a. A car normally has five of these including reverse _____

b. Easy to understand _____

c. To look for something that is difficult to find _____

Group B
a. Sincere and serious _____

b. The planet we live on _____

c. Hair grown on a man's chin and cheeks _____

Group C
a. 1990, 1991 and 1992 are all _____.

b. To recognise or understand sounds _____

   c. A violent movement of the ground _____

Group D
   a. Not quite, almost _____

   b. A sweet juicy fruit _____

   c. The opposite of front _____

2   One of the words in each group is pronounced differently from the others. Which is it
and how is it pronounced? How are the other words pronounced?

The combination **ei** is usually pronounced in two ways:

   /iː/   (*eg*: deceive receipt)
   /eɪ/   (*eg*: eight neighbour)

It can also be pronounced:

   /aɪ/   (*eg*: height)
   /e/   (*eg*: leisure)
   /ə/   (*eg*: foreign)

> *But be careful!*
> These two words can be pronounced in two ways:
>   either /ɪː/ or /aɪ/
>   neither /ɪː/ or /aɪ/

PRACTICE

Use the words in the box to fill in the spaces in the sentences below. A word that rhymes
with the correct answer has been underlined to help you.

> eighty   weight   reign   height   freight   foreign   leisure   veils   vein
>
> neighbour

1   In some countries females wear _____

2   Put that <u>crate</u> in the room marked _____

3   I <u>hate</u> putting on _____. I shouldn't eat so much.

4   My Aunt <u>Katie</u> celebrated her birthday today. She's _____!

5   Pudding <u>Lane</u> has been called that since the _____ of Queen Elizabeth I.

6   The _____ of the ceiling makes this room seem very <u>light</u>.

7   The <u>florin</u> is a _____ coin.

8   It's a <u>pleasure</u> to use the _____ centre.

9   My _____ always votes <u>Labour</u>.

10   The jugular _____ is the <u>main</u> one taking blood from the <u>brain</u>.

12

g

The letter **g** is usually pronounced:

/g/   (*eg*: magazine glass great)

However, when **g** is followed by **e** it is usually pronounced:

/dʒ/   (*eg*: change age geography)

and in the following common words the pronunciation is also /dʒ/:

apology engineer giant gypsy origin religion

> ***But be careful!***
> There are some common exceptions where **g** before **e** is pronounced /g/
> (*eg*: tiger get gear hamburger).

gu is usually pronounced /g/. For example:

guard guest synagogue figure

There are a few exceptions, mostly words of Spanish origin, which are pronounced /gw/. For example:

guacamole guava guano

(See also the pronunciation of **ng** and **ough**.)

PRACTICE

1 Match the words in the box to the definitions in groups below.

> lodger huge oxygen angry badge vegetables cigar bargain fridge
>
> legs gallon agree bridge guilty cage beggar

Group A
a. A machine for keeping food cold _____

b. Something that you buy very cheaply _____

c. We have two, other animals have four! _____

d. The opposite of *innocent* _____

Group B
a. Feeling upset or annoyed about something _____

b. A secure place for a dangerous animal _____

c. Extremely large _____

d. We need to breathe this to live _____

Group C
a. A structure allowing us to cross a river by foot _____

b. A symbol we wear to show our name or position _____

c. To have the same opinion as someone else _____

d. Peas, beans and carrots are all _____

2 One of the words in each group is pronounced differently from the others. Which is it and how is it pronounced? How are the other words pronounced?

13

ie

ie is usually pronounced:

/iː/   (*eg*: chief field)

It can also be pronounced:

/e/   (*eg*: friend)
/ə/   (*eg*: conscience)

It can also be pronounced as a diphthong:

/ɪə/   (*eg*: convenience fierce)
/aɪə/   (*eg*: quiet science)
/juː/   (*eg*: view)
/aɪ/   (*eg*: die)

PRACTICE

I   Match the words in the box to the definitions in groups.

> audience   niece   friendship   proficiency   efficient   review   scientist
>
> impatience   twentieth   ancient   conscience   relief   experience   diet
>
> society   series

Group A
a. A person who works in chemistry, physics, etc. _____

b. A programme of controlling how much you eat _____

c. A large group of people who share customs and laws _____

d. Extremely old _____

Group B
a. People watching or listening to a performance _____

b. Something that happens to you and affects you _____

c. The century we are living in now _____

d. The feeling of being unable to wait for something _____

Group C

a. The daughter of your brother or sister is your _____

b. A feeling of comfort after pain or anxiety _____

c. A number of connected things _____

d. An article giving an opinion about a book or film _____

Group D

a. A feeling between persons who like each other _____

b. A sense of right and wrong _____

c. Working well or economically _____

d. The quality of being good at something _____

2   One of the words in each group is pronounced differently from the others. Which is it and how is it pronounced? How are the other words pronounced?

14

ng

When **ng** is at the end of a word or stem it is normally pronounced:

/ŋ/   (*eg:* reading song singer)

However, in the middle of a word it is often pronounced:

/ŋg/   (*eg:* hunger hungry single)

When **ng** is followed by **e**, it is often pronounced:

/ndʒ/   (*eg:* strange challenge)

When it follows **th**, some people pronounce it:

/k/   (*eg:* length strength)

PRACTICE

1   Label these pictures using the words below:

> king   hanger   finger   messenger   wrong

a. _____   b. _____   c. _____   d. _____   e. _____

2   Match the words in the box to the definitions in groups below.

> belong   strongest   danger   long   stranger   wrong   longer   hungry   young
>
> change   sting   ringing

Group A
  a. The opposite of *short* _____

  b. Can you hear the phone _____? I'll have to answer it.

  c. To feel a sharp pain _____

  d. To become something different _____

Group B
  a. Wanting food _____

  b. The most powerful _____

  c. The possibility of being hurt or in trouble _____

  d. Having more length _____

Group C
  a. To be part of a group _____

  b. The opposite of *old* _____

  c. This isn't correct, it's _____

  d. A person who isn't known in a particular place _____

3   One of the words in each group is pronounced differently from the others. Which is it
and how is it pronounced? How are the other words pronounced?

oa

There are two common ways to pronounce **oa**:

/əʊ/ (*eg:* boat road coal)
/ɔ:/ (*eg:* roar broad)

PRACTICE

1 Label the pictures using the words in the box below.

| soap   oar   oak   goat   toast   coat   loaf   foal   goal |

a. _____   b. _____   c. _____   d. _____   e. _____

f. _____   g. _____   h. _____   i. _____

2 Except for one of these words, **oa** has the same sound. Which word is different and how is it pronounced?

3 Match the words in the box to the definitions in groups underneath.

| broadcast   blackboard   roast   load   abroad   approach   boast
cardboard   loan |

Group A

a. In another country _____

b. A teacher writes on this with chalk _____

c. To come near to something _____

Group B

a. A programme on TV or radio _____

b. To talk about yourself in a proud way _____

c. Something carried by a vehicle or animal _____

Group C

a. What boxes are usually made of _____

b. Money lent to someone _____

c. To cook meat in an oven _____

4   One of the words in each group is pronounced differently from the others. Which is it and how is it pronounced? How are the other words pronounced?

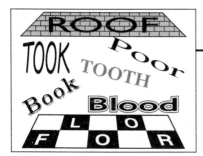

16
oo

The combination **oo** is usually pronounced in two ways:

/ʊ/   (eg: book foot)
/uː/ (eg: boot fool)

> *But be careful!*
> There are some common exceptions (eg: blood /ʌ/   door /ɔː/   poor /ʊə/)

PRACTICE

1   Label the pictures on the next page using the words in the box below.

> bookshelf   moon   pool   football   cooker   school

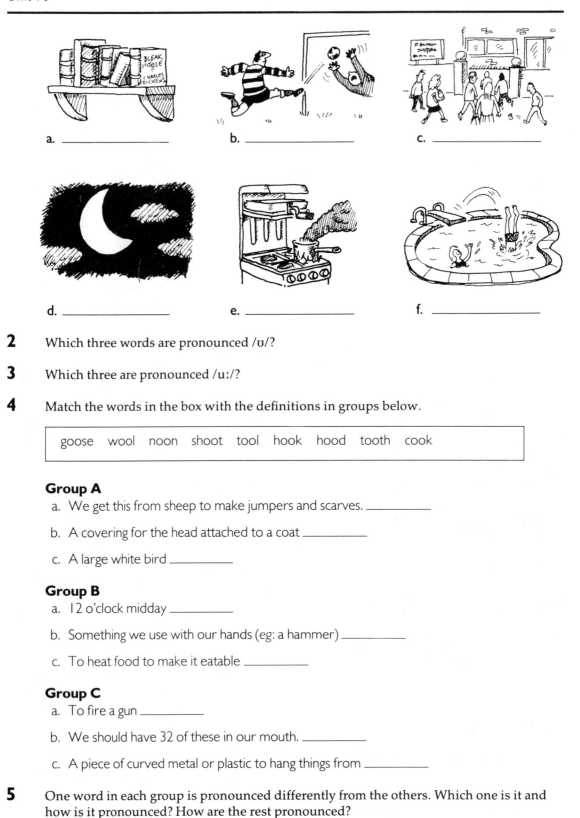

a. _____

b. _____

c. _____

d. _____

e. _____

f. _____

2   Which three words are pronounced /ʊ/?

3   Which three are pronounced /uː/?

4   Match the words in the box with the definitions in groups below.

goose   wool   noon   shoot   tool   hook   hood   tooth   cook

Group A
a. We get this from sheep to make jumpers and scarves. _____

b. A covering for the head attached to a coat _____

c. A large white bird _____

Group B
a. 12 o'clock midday _____

b. Something we use with our hands (eg: a hammer) _____

c. To heat food to make it eatable _____

Group C
a. To fire a gun _____

b. We should have 32 of these in our mouth. _____

c. A piece of curved metal or plastic to hang things from _____

5   One word in each group is pronounced differently from the others. Which one is it and how is it pronounced? How are the rest pronounced?

or

The combination **or** is normally pronounced:

/ɔ:/ (*eg*: for horse corner)

It can also be pronounced:

/ɜ:/ (*eg*: work worse worship world worm world)

However, when **or** is unstressed it is usually pronounced:

/ə/ (*eg*: dȯctor cȯmfort)

In some common words it is also pronounced:

/ɒ/ (*eg*: moral forest foreign corridor horoscope orange orient)

And in a few words it is pronounced:

/ʌ/ (*eg*: worry thorough)

PRACTICE

1 Label the pictures below using the words in the box.

> orchestra   anchor   equator   organ   cork   forty

a. _____   b. _____   c. _____   d. _____   e. _____   f. _____

2 Which four are pronounced /ɔ:/?

3 Which two are pronounced /ə/?

4 Match the words in the box with the definitions on the next page.

> horrible   order   world   border   correct   forest   more   sailor   work

a. Something you are paid to do

b. A Rolls Royce costs _____ than a Ford.

c. A large piece of land covered in trees

d. Synonym for terrible

e. A dividing line between countries

f. The opposite of *wrong*

g. To tell someone to do something

h. Someone who works on a ship

i. The earth

5 How is the **or** pronounced in each of these words?

18
ou

In stressed syllables the most common way of pronouncing **ou** is:

/aʊ/ (*eg*: about house plough)

Two other common ways are:

/ʌ/ (*eg*: young rough)
/uː/ (*eg*: you soup)

In unstressed syllables **ou** is normally pronounced:

(*eg*/ə/moustache flavour dangerous)

> *But be careful!*
> Here are some common exceptions:
> /ɔː/ (*eg*: ought pour)
> /əʊ/ (*eg*: soul although)
> /ʊ/ (*eg*: could would)

(See also the sections on the pronunciation of **ough** and **our**.)

PRACTICE

1   Label the pictures using the words in the box below.

> pound   souvenir   mountain   soup   cloud   couple   fountain   mouth
>
> mouse

a. _____   b. _____   c. _____   d. _____   e. _____

f. _____   g. _____   h. _____   i. _____

2   Two of the words are pronounced /uː/. Which are they?

3   One of the words is pronounced /ʌ/. Which is it?

4   Match the words in the box with the definitions in groups below.

> countries   count   loud   route   wound   account   south   double   cousins
>
> through   lounge   sound

Group A
   a. To say numbers in order (eg: 1 2 3 4 . . .) _____

   b. East, west, north and _____

   c. A planned direction for a walk or journey _____

Group B
   a. England, Japan and Nigeria are all _____

   b. Your uncle or aunt's children are your _____

   c. A comfortable room for sitting in _____

Group C

a. A written or spoken record, especially of numbers _____

b. Something you hear _____

c. Something that is exactly the same as something else _____

Group D

a. An injury to the body _____

b. Moving into and out of a space _____

c. Opposite of *quiet* _____

5 One word in each group is pronounced differently from the others. Which one is it and how is it pronounced? How are the rest pronounced?

 | 19

ough

The combination **ough** has many different pronunciations:

/ɒf/ (*eg:* cough)
/ʌf/ (*eg:* enough tough rough)
/uː/ (*eg:* through)
/aʊ/ (*eg:* bough plough)
/ə/ (*eg:* thorough borough)
/ɔː/ (*eg:* brought bought thought ought)
/əʊ/ (*eg:* although dough)

PRACTICE

Complete the poem using the words above and the rhymes to help you.

A Cruise

The wind got up, the sea got _____

And very soon we'd had _____

Some caught colds and started to _____

We just wanted to get off.

The captain said we must be _____

Sailors are of stronger stuff.

But then at last the sun came _____

And then we felt as good as new.

Just two more days to get to port

We packed the presents that we'd _____

We sighted land, a horse and a _____

Nearly home, we were happy now.

20

our

In stressed syllables **our** is normally pronounced in two ways:

/aʊə/   (*eg*: our flour)
/ɔː/   (*eg*: course tour)

There is one common exception:

/ʌ/   courage

In unstressed syllables **our** is normally pronounced:

/ə/   (*eg*: harbour behaviour)

PRACTICE

I   Match the words in the box with the definitions on the next page.

court   sour   resource   source   neighbour   hour   tourist   yours   four

a. A place where matters of law are decided _____

b. Someone visiting a country for pleasure _____

c. The opposite of *sweet* _____

d. Something that belongs to you is _____

e. One, two, three, _____

f. Something natural a country has that is very valuable (eg: coal, gas, diamonds) _____

g. The point from which something comes (eg: a river) _____

h. Sixty minutes = one _____

i. A person who lives next door _____

2   How is the **our** pronounced in each of these words?

21

OW

There are two common ways to pronounce **ow**:

/aʊ/ (*eg*: how towel crowd)
/əʊ/ (*eg*: below show pillow)

> **But be careful!**
> There is a small group of words that can be pronounced in either way, depending on their meaning (see 'Homographs' later in this book). The most common are *bow*, *row* and *sow*.
>
> Also note that the **ow** in *towards* is pronounced /uː/.

PRACTICE

1   Label the pictures on the next page using the words in the box below.

crown   bowl   arrow   shower   snow   tower

a. _____ b. _____ c. _____ d. _____ e. _____ f. _____

2 Which three are pronounced /aʊ/?

3 Which three are pronounced /əʊ/?

4 Match the words in the box with the definitions in groups below.

> sorrow   yellow   own   drown   power   allow   low   flower   mow   cow
>
> town   now

Group A
   a. A large female animal that gives milk _____

   b. At the moment _____

   c. The opposite of *high* _____

Group B
   a. Great sadness _____

   b. The colour of the sun, a banana, etc. _____

   c. To let someone do something _____

Group C
   a. If something belongs to you, you _____ it.

   b. To die by being unable to breathe under water _____

   c. Smaller than a city, larger than a village _____

Group D
   a. The ability, skill or opportunity to do something _____

   b. To cut grass with a machine _____

   c. A brightly coloured part of a plant _____

5 One word in each group is pronounced differently from the others. Which one is it and how is it pronounced? How are the rest pronounced?

qu(e)

The combination **qu** is generally pronounced:

/kw/ (*eg*: queen liquid)

There are some common exceptions, where it is pronounced:

/k/ (*eg*: quiche quay conquer bouquet liquor mosquito)

When **que** is found at the *end* of a word, it is also pronounced:

/k/ (*eg*: cheque)

PRACTICE

1 Put the following words into the correct categories.

> question unique frequent square antique request squeeze equal
>
> quarrel quarter

	/kw/	/k/
_____	_____	_____
_____	_____	_____
_____	_____	
_____	_____	

2 Now use these words to fill in the sentences below.

a. A shape with four sides of the same length is a _____

b. Another way of saying *the same* length is _____ length.

c. You ask someone a _____ to get information.

d. If you divide something by four you get four _____

e. An old and valuable piece of furniture is called an _____

f. When you make a _____ to someone, you ask them to do something for you.

g. To get water out of a sponge you must _____ it.

h. Another word for a *row* or *argument* is a _____

i. _____ is another way of saying *often* or *regular*.

j. If something is _____ it is the only one of its kind.

3 Practice saying these sentences quickly!

a. Quick liquor and quiet quiche frequently.

b. The liquid squid questions the quarrelling queen mosquito.

23

th

At the beginning of a word **th** is usually pronounced:

/θ/ (*eg:* thing Thursday theatre)

There are the following common exceptions, pronounced /ð/:

than that the their then them there they these those though this

In the middle of a word **th** is usually pronounced:

/ð/ (*eg:* father clothing other)

There are the following common exceptions, pronounced /θ/:

athletics authority author nothing something mathematics method

At the end of a word **th** is usually pronounced:

/θ/ (*eg:* cloth breath bath)

There are the following common exceptions, pronounced /ð/:

with smooth breathe

In a few words **th** is also pronounced:

/t/ (*eg:* Thames Thailand thyme Thomas)

PRACTICE

I   Label the pictures using the words in the box below.

| three   bath   feather   thumb   tooth   thousand   thermometer |

a. _____   b. _____   c. _____   d. _____

e. _____   f. _____   g. _____

2   Which six are pronounced /θ/?

3   Which one is pronounced /ð/?

4   Match the words in the box with the definitions in groups below.

| thorough   gather   furthest   months   health   through   with   bathroom rhythm   weather   athletics   although |

Group A
a. Moving in and out of space _____

b. Complete, carefully done _____

c. However, but _____

Group B
a. January, February and March are all _____

b. The condition of being free from illness _____

c. I stayed _____ my family over the summer _____

Group C
a. The place in your house where you wash yourself _____

b. Climate _____

c. Regular movement or musical beat _____

Group D

a. Track and field sports _____

b. The longest distance from here _____

c. To bring together _____

5 One word in each group is pronounced differently from the others. Which one is it and how is it pronounced? How are the rest pronounced?

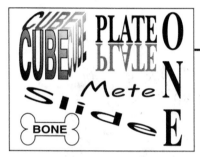

24

Adding e

Normally in one-syllable words, a single vowel followed by a single consonant is a short vowel:

/ɪ/	(*eg:* bit)
/æ/	(*eg:* rat)
/ɒ/	(*eg:* cod)
/ʌ/	(*eg:* cut)
/e/	(*eg:* met)

If the consonant is followed by an **e**, then the vowel is usually a diphthong:

/aɪ/	(*eg:* bite)
/eɪ/	(*eg:* rate)
/əʊ/	(*eg:* code)

However, in the case of **u** or **e** + a consonant, a long vowel is formed when we add **e**:

/u:/	(*eg:* cute)
/i:/	(*eg:* mete)

> *But be careful!*
> There are exceptions in the pronunciation of some common words (*eg:* one /wʌn/ some /sʌm/)

PRACTICE

Complete the poem using the rhymes and some of the words in the box to help you.

fin / fine	hat / hate	not / note
win / wine	fat / fate	hop / hope
pin / pine	plan / plane	
nil / nile	can / cane	
shin / shine	cap / cape	
kit / kite		

The Race

They climbed on up through woods of _____

High above the River Rhine.

They'd brought their lunch but not a map,

They'd got some plates but not a _____.

The air was cool but the weather was _____.

They ate their food and drank their _____.

After the meal they thought of a _____

To see who was quickest, woman or _____.

'Get to the bottom as fast as you _____.

One, two, three, go, and off they ran.

The man went left and trusted to _____

Down a steep path – 'At the bottom, I'll wait.

He suddenly fell and hit his _____.

'If this goes on, I'll never _____.

He couldn't walk, he had to _____

And every few steps he had to stop.

The woman turned right, and said 'I _____

This is the way down the easier slope.'

It started to rain and she hadn't a _____.

She wore a small plate and was happy with that.

In the woods in the valley, the sun didn't _____.

She looked for her man but there wasn't a sign.

She took out some paper and wrote him a _____:

'I'm sorry, must go or I'll miss the last boat'.

When the man got there the woman was _____.

He was weary and wet, and his leg hurt a lot.

'I must exercise more, to be properly fit.

I'll get into trainers and buy all the _____.'

The game is all over and the score is one _____

But he's still hopping madly around that big hill.

25

Final se

At the end of a word **se** is normally pronounced either /s/ or /z/. We can often predict which to use by the sound before.

It is generally pronounced /s/ after:

/ɜ:/	(*eg:* nurse)
/aʊ/	(*eg:* mouse)
/ɪ/	(*eg:* promise)
/ə/	(*eg:* purpose)
/n/	(*eg:* sense)

It is generally pronounced /z/ after:

/aɪ/	(*eg:* rise)
/ɔɪ/	(*eg:* noise)
/ɑ:/	(*eg:* vase)

There are four vowel sounds where **se** is pronounced either /s/ or /z/, depending on the particular word:

/eɪ/ (*eg:* base /s/ raise /z/)
/uː/ (*eg:* loose /s/ lose /z/)
/iː/ (*eg:* increase /s/ please /z/)
/ɔː/ (*eg:* horse /s/ cause /z/)

After the sound /aʊ/ **se** can be pronounced /s/ or /z/, depending upon what part of speech the word is; for example:

/s/ A *close* thing [adjective]
Close by was a farm. [adverb]
She lives in a *close*. [noun]
/z/ *Close* the door. [verb]

/s/ The *use* of arms is banned. [noun]
/z/ *Use* the blue pen. [verb]

/s/ He worked as a *refuse* collector. [noun]
/z/ I *refuse* to do it. [verb]

/s/ Her *excuse* was accepted. [noun]
/z/ *Excuse* me! [verb]

The pronunciation of these words is often confused:

/s/ Did you *loose* the tigers from the cage? [verb (meaning to set free)]
Leave your hair *loose*. [adjective]
/z/ When did you *lose* it? [verb]

PRACTICE

I Complete the sentences below using the words in the box. Use the rhyming words underlined to help you.

course erase expense cheese pause goose wise choose chase
release nose promise

a. I hate it when lifts _____ between <u>floors</u>.

b. The policeman had a red <u>face</u> after giving _____ to the thief.

c. He was sunburnt all over from the tip of his _____ to his <u>toes</u>.

d. Her face went <u>puce</u> red when you called her a _____

e. I think our neighbours should share the _____ of the new <u>fence</u>.

f. Now we have <u>peace</u>, they should _____ all the prisoners of war.

g. Don't tell me lies about how _____ he is!

h. If you take me to the Palace I _____ to be good.

i. We always watch the news when you _____ the TV programme.

j. If you go through the X-rays they might _____ your film!

k. Of _____ you could always force open the door.

l. He's very fond of French food, especially their _____

2 Label the pictures below using the words in the box.

mouse nurse bruise noise purse rose blouse applause

a. _____ b. _____ c. _____ d. _____

e. _____ f. _____ g. _____ h. _____

3 Which five are pronounced /z/?

4 Which three are pronounced /s/?

s and es in plurals and third person verbs

Normally **s** and **es** are pronounced either /s/, /z/ or /ɪz/, depending upon the final sound of the root word.

They are pronounced /z/ after the following consonant sounds:

	Plural nouns	Third person verbs
/b/	cubs	Kate robs banks.
/v/	caves	He lives in Hove.
/ð/	clothes	She bathes her feet.
/d/	beds	He reads *The Times*.
/g/	eggs	She digs the garden.
/l/	hills	It fills the room.
/m/	rooms	He comes today.
/n/	pens	She learns French.
/ŋ/	rings	It brings the rain.

They are also pronounced /z/ after words ending in *any* vowel sound; for example:

	Plural nouns	Third person verbs
/əʊ/	potatoes	She goes jogging.
/eɪ/	days	He plays tennis.
/eə/	hairs	She wears black.

s and **es** are pronounced /s/ after the following consonant sounds:

	Plural nouns	Third person verbs
/p/	cups	It escapes me.
/f/	cuffs	She laughs a lot.
/θ/	cloths	She baths the baby.
/t/	coats	It lights the room.
/k/	banks	It breaks the law.

They are pronounced /ɪz/ after the following consonant sounds:

	Plural nouns	Third person verbs
/s/	buses	He advises people.
/ʃ/	wishes	She fishes on Sunday.
/z/	roses	He loses his temper.
/dʒ/	marriages	It encourages them.
/tʃ/	watches	She catches the ball.
/ks/	boxes	TV relaxes me.

PRACTICE

1 List the following words in the right group according to the pronunciation of **s** and **es** in plural or third person forms.

church   add   burn   baby   carpet   beer   cage   break   build   leave   face
garage   fork   dress   kick   hold   door   jet   fox   law   make   need   pass
plant   myth   nose   milk   seagull   pig   night   market   meeting   swim
ring   start   sell   stamp   wind   voice   suit   week   record   thing   shape
programme   tree   train   turn   take   talk   rain   wait   proof   smooth

Group 1: /z/

_____

_____

_____

_____

Group 2: /s/

_____

_____

_____

Group 3: /ɪz/

_____

_____

2   Match the words in the box with the groups of definitions below.

> students   paths   jobs   glasses   writes   letters   dogs   heads   stops
>
> doors   cooks   babies   finishes   does   asks   teaches   machines   washes

Group A
a. People whose job is to prepare food _____

b. He always _____ questions but never answers them.

c. Four-legged pets you take for a walk _____

Group B
a. People learning at university _____

b. Tracks to walk along _____

c. People in charge (eg: at school) _____

Group C
a. Teacher, bus driver and waiter are all _____

b. Very young humans _____

c. Places to get on or off a bus or train _____

Group D
a. The lesson starts at 10 and _____ at 10.50.

b. Mr Brown _____ maths at the high school.

c. Pieces of equipment (eg: photocopier, printing press) _____

Group E
a. Transparent containers we drink from _____

b. My cat is very clean and _____ itself every day.

c. He _____ not know the answer.

Group F
a. Fred _____ stories for the television.

b. A, B, C, D are all _____

c. Used to close the entrance to a room or building _____

3   One word in each group is pronounced differently from the others. Which one is it and how is it pronounced? How are the rest pronounced?

Final y

In one-syllable words where **y** follows a consonant, it is pronounced:

/aɪ/   (*eg*: why fly)

In multi-syllable words where **y** follows **f**, it is also pronounced:

/aɪ/   (*eg*: modify simplify)

and in the following common words:

deny reply rely apply supply July multiply

In other multi-syllable words, **y** following a consonant is normally pronounced:

/iː/   (*eg*: many equality)

After a vowel **y** is pronounced according to the sound it follows:

/eɪ/   (*eg*: pay display)
/ɔɪ/   (*eg*: boy annoy)
/iː/   (*eg*: key money)
/aɪ/   (*eg*: buy)

PRACTICE

I   Complete the poem using the words in the box.

fly   my   cry   shy   by   try   why

Babies _____

Children ask _____

Kids are _____

Parents _____

And in _____ life

The years _____ _____

2   Find the three words in which **y** is *not* pronounced /i:/. Use these words to complete the sentence below.

ugly	lucky	heavy	empty	funny	quality	dignity	hurry	carry	apply
worry	duty	qualify	company	whisky	anniversary	century	July		
quantity	monkey	happily	quickly	wealthy	identity				

To _____ for the job which will be vacant in _____, you first need to _____

as a teacher.

28

Past endings

The regular past ending **ed** can normally be pronounced in three ways, depending upon the final sound of the root word:

/d/   after voiced sounds (*eg*: opened)
      after vowel sounds (*eg*: covered)

/t/   after unvoiced sounds (*eg*: stopped)

/ɪd/ after /d/ or /t/ (*eg*: posted   needed)

There is a small group of verbs that have both irregular and regular forms and pronunciation:

/d/   dreamed   learned   burned
/t/   dreamt   learnt   burnt

PRACTICE

Look at the final sound of each of the words in the box and put them into the correct category.

accept act add admire agree allow answer appear approach
argue arrive attack attend attract avoid bath bathe call climb
clothe compare connect continue control cough crash cross dance
defend deliver demand depend describe destroy die disturb drag
drop educate empty enjoy enter excite explain fail fetch fold
follow frighten hire hope imagine improve inform join jump
laugh like love manage mend name notice organise pack
persuade play pour promise pull reach receive relax remember
repair reply rub shop show start visit walk wash

Unvoiced sounds:

_____

_____

_____

/d/ or /t/:

_____

_____

_____

Vowel sounds:

_____

_____

_____

Voiced sounds:

_____

_____

_____

Shifting stress in two-syllable words

Most two-syllable words do not change their stress patterns when they are used as different parts of speech. For example:

Your glass is empty. [adjective]
Please empty your pockets. [verb]

Travel broadens the mind. [noun]
I want to travel around the world before I die. [verb]

However, there is a group of common words that *do* change their stress pattern when they are used as different parts of speech. In general, nouns are stressed on the first syllable and verbs on the second syllable. For example:

He kept a record of his journeys. [noun]
I want to record this for my grandchildren to see. [verb]

PRACTICE

Complete the sentences below by choosing the word which has the correct stress.

1 A _____ is a place where very little grows.   a. desert   b. desert

2 Soldiers who _____ the army will be shot.

3 English spelling can _____ problems.   a. present   b. present

4 My colleagues gave me an expensive _____ when I left
   the company.

5 What is the _____ of this sentence?   a. object   b. object

6 Many people _____ to people smoking in public places.

7 The company _____ the machines to Europe.   a. exports   b. exports

8 _____ last year went up by 10 per cent.

9 _____ of foreign goods have fallen.   a. imports   b. imports

10 Any company which _____ goods must complete the
   Customs forms.

11 The cost of living seems to _____ daily.   a. increase   b. increase

84

12 The government has announced an _____ in taxation.

13 The _____ was in my name.

14 Please _____ all the money into my deposit account.

    a. tránsfer   b. transfér

15 The exercises _____ from easy to difficult.

16 He made good _____ last term.

    a. prógress   b. progréss

17 You need a _____ to park here.

18 The hotel rules do not _____ visitors after 11 o'clock.

    a. pérmit   b. permít

19 French _____ includes wine and cheese.

20 What does your country _____?

    a. próduce   b. prodúce

21 My next _____ will be an electric car.

22 Opera singers can _____ their voices to reach the whole audience.

    a. próject   b. projéct

23 Companies _____ their goods by train or lorry.

24 The most environmentally friendly means of _____ is the bicycle.

    a. tránsport   b. transpórt

25 Lewes Town caused an _____ by knocking Arsenal out of the Cup.

26 He _____ his sister by breaking her new toy.

    a. úpset   b. upsét

27 I _____ that he is not all that he appears to be.

28 The police have arrested a _____ for the murder.

    a. súspect   b. suspéct

29 My _____ allows me to have eight weeks' holiday.

30 We usually _____ auxiliary verbs in spoken English.

    a. contráct   b. cóntract

31 The _____ of her talk was very interesting.

32 The Customs must _____ all passengers to a thorough search.

    a. subjéct   b. súbject

33 I noticed the _____ between London and the village where I grew up.

34 I want to _____ the lives of the rich and the poor in the city.

    a. cóntrast   b. contrást

Silent letters

Some words contain letters that are not pronounced. These letters can be at the beginning of words; for example:

pneumonia honest

They can be at the end of words; for example:

bomb hymn

Or they can be in the middle of words; for example:

straight castle

In words beginning with **wh**, the **h** is usually silent; for example:

why which

However, there are a few words where the **w** is silent:

who whole

PRACTICE

I   Complete the spelling of the words by adding the silent letters. Use only the letters in the box.

> k p h g b w n

a. ___sychology is the study of the mind.

b. An ___onest person never steals anything.

c. ___hose shoes are those? Oh, they're mine.

d. He hurt his ___nee when he fell over.

e. A bom___ exploded near the centre of town.

f. A ___nat is like a very small mosquito.

g. The spirit of a dead person is called a g___ost.

h. I ___now I need new ___nitting needles.

i. Did you hear someone ___nock at the door?

j. His __nowledge of films is very extensive.

k. A hym__ is a religious song.

l. He lived in a very cold house and caught __neumonia.

m. I read the __hole book in a day.

n. The bell rings every __our.

o. __ho are you talking to?

p. I'm sorry, I'm __rong and you're right.

q. Don't clim__ the mountain today, it's too foggy.

r. He was a __sychopath who killed ten people.

s. I must __rap her present up before she comes home.

t. He tied a __not in his handkerchief so he wouldn't forget.

2 Complete the spelling of the words by adding the silent letters. Use only the letters in the box.

b p c n l h t gh d r w

a. It's hard teaching this class – ha__f of them don't lis__en.

b. You must visit the cas__le by ni__t.

c. Keep your recei__t – you may need to take the machine back to the shop.

d. No dou__t you will meet him soon.

e. We ta__ked while we wa__ked.

f. I got a box of han__kerchiefs for Chris__mas.

g. Every We__nesday I take a san__wich to work because the canteen is closed.

h. You'll find the cha__k in the cu__board.

i. Don't tell me the ans__er yet.

j. My mus__les hurt after a lot of exercise.

k. I love these pa__m trees along the beach.

l. The passengers kept ca__m during the fli__t.

m. He cut off the king's head with his s__ord.

n. S__ience is the study of chemistry and physics.

o. The gover__ment of Britain meets at the Houses of Parliament.

p. The ex＿aust on your ve＿icle is illegal.

q. Could you i＿on my shirt please, mum?

r. Only the sta＿ks of corn are left after the harvest.

s. She sang some old fo＿k songs from her country.

t. He went out of business owing thousands of pounds in de＿ts.

31

Silent syllables

Some words seem on paper to have more syllables than when they are pronounced, because one of the syllables is usually dropped when speaking.

Most silent syllables occur after a stressed syllable. In the following examples the stressed syllable is marked with a square and the silent syllable is underlined.

> She sat down in a comfortable armchair and watched television. That evening she watched the news with reports from the political conferences and then an interesting programme on cooking unusual vegetables.

However, in the group of words ending in **ry** and **ly**, it is always the second-last syllable that is dropped, wherever the stress occurs in the word.

> Last night I watched a documentary on a typically ordinary family. The husband worked in a factory and his wife worked in a public library. It made me angry that it was her that bought the groceries every day.

PRACTICE

Which syllables are dropped in the words underlined?

1 My <u>favourite</u> type of music is <u>opera</u>.

2 The <u>average</u> <u>national</u> <u>temperature</u> is <u>moderate</u> at this time of year.

3 Have you seen my <u>camera</u>?

4 *The <u>History</u> of <u>Capitalism</u> and <u>Machinery</u>* is published by <u>Boundary</u> Press.

5 <u>Every</u> person in the <u>launderette</u> looked <u>miserable</u>.

6 It's a <u>mystery</u> how she does it! She's with a <u>different</u> man each time I see her.

7 This <u>dictionary</u> tells you the <u>history</u> of each word.

8 The <u>missionary</u> told of the <u>flavouring</u> <u>necessary</u> for the <u>cookery</u> practised by the local tribes.

9 What's <u>happening</u> at the <u>surgery</u>?

10 In <u>general</u>, people have <u>several</u> different jobs in their lives.

11 He's looking forward <u>hopefully</u> to <u>victory</u> in his next match.

 | # 32

Homographs

Some words have the same spelling, but have two very different pronunciations. For example:

lead
/li:d/ – the verb meaning the opposite of *to follow*
/led/ – a type of metal

PRACTICE

Complete the pairs of sentences on the next page by choosing the word in the right hand column which rhymes with the word underlined.

Example

1 Row the _____ across the river.

  a. now /aʊ/   b. boat /əʊ/

2 We mustn't have a <u>row</u> _____ in front of the children – they don't like us arguing.

Answer: 1 b. 2 a.

3 When you _____ your watch, you'll need to <u>wind</u> it up.

  a. find /aɪ/   b. thinned /ɪ/

4 The strong <u>wind</u> _____ his hair.

5 You must take _____ not to <u>tear</u> that dress.

  a. near /ɪə/   b. care /eə/

6 When she cried, a <u>tear</u> fell _____ his hand.

7 _____ many times must I <u>bow</u> to the king?

  a. go /əʊ/   b. how /aʊ/

8 _____ and put on a <u>bow</u> tie – it's a very formal occasion.

9 I _____ to <u>read</u> the newspapers in my job.

  a. need /iː/   b. bed /e/

10 Yesterday I <u>read</u> all the papers in _____

11 <u>Close</u> the door before he _____

  a. goes /z/   b. most /s/

12 _____ shops are very <u>close</u>.

13 It's no <u>use</u>, there isn't enough _____

  a. shoes /z/   b. mousse /s/

14 <u>Use</u> my _____

15 He <u>lives</u> on the money his father _____ him.

  a. drives /aɪ/   b. gives /ɪ/

16 The way he _____, he needs nine <u>lives</u>!

17 The _____ live in the same barn as the <u>sows</u>.

  a. mows /əʊ/   b. cows /aʊ/

18 The farmer _____ the field and then <u>sows</u> the seed in it.

Answer Key

Part 1

1. /iː/ (1)

1

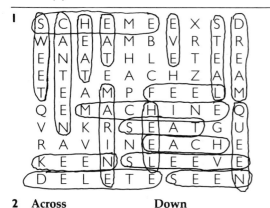

2

Across	Down
a. scheme	a. sweet
b. athlete	b. canteen
c. teach	c. heat
d. team	d. eat
e. feel	e. marine
f. machine	f. heel
g. seat	g. Eve
h. ravine	h. steal
i. each	i. dream
j. keen	j. queen
k. sleeve	
l. delete	
m. seen	

3 brief piece relief believe field
receive hygiene deceive perceive
chiefly protein

2. /ɔː/ (3)

1 paws claws jaws pause thought
2 a – 5
     b – 8
     c – 7
     d – 10
     e – 2
     f – 12
     g – 4
     h – 11
     i – 9
     j – 6
     k – 1
     l – 3

3

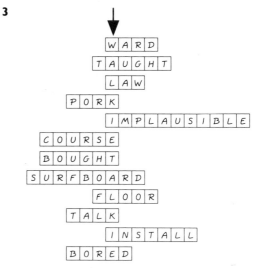

Mystery word: Walkie-talkie

3. /uː/ (5)

1

2

Across	Down
a. off duty	a. stupid
b. suitcase	b. computer
c. value	c. noon
d. opportunity	d. issue
e. pursue	e. into
f. usual	f. view
g. pew	g. chew
h. boot	h. shoe
i. zoo	i. humour
j. producer	j. loosen
k. use	k. argue
l. newsagent	l. unite
m. choose	
n. huge	

4. /ʌ/ (7)

1 honey	**4** curry	**7** none	**10** dove
2 money	**5** worry	**8** tonne	**11** love
3 sunny	**6** hurry	**9** son	**12** some
			13 come

5. /ə/ *(8)*

1

afraid	data	tonight
sugar	father	mirror
statement	important	centre
employment	nation	dignity
human	status	helpfully
figure		

2 A hundred photographers from Canada and America arrived in Britain to join the discussion in London about the role of television and newspapers when reporting from war zones. There has so far been no agreement with governments on abolishing visa controls or on providing significant improvements in consular assistance abroad.

6. /ɪə/ *(9)*

Dear Members of Staff

It *appears* that as the end of the *year* comes *nearer* we will need some *volunteers* to help the *cashiers* at the check-out. I hope this will not *interfere* with your holiday plans.

Also, according to the *engineer*, it is *clear* that the damage to the machines is due to the *severe* temperatures *we're* having at the moment, so please cover your machines when you leave the office.

Yours *sincerely*

J D De Vere

7. /eɪ/ *(10)*

Dear *Jane*

How was your *holiday* in the *States*? It's a nice *place* to have a *break*, isn't it? I hope you weren't too *afraid*. So many people *say* New York is a *crazy* city but I couldn't *complain* about my own *stay* in the USA. I felt quite *safe*.

I went on an *exchange* visit with a friend at school who was the *same age*. His father was a *painter* called *David Cape*. I remember that his favourite meal was *steak* and chips.

What was the weather like? When I was there we had a lot of *rain*. Especially the *day* we went to a *game* of baseball. They had to stop it. I didn't mind as no-one could *explain* it to me *anyway*!

Must go now. I've got a *train* to catch. I *may* have a new job in TV. I'm still in search of *fame*!

Lots of love

Lorraine

8. /aɪ/ *(11)*

1 bicycle	6 giant	11 Friday	16 Irish
2 cyclist	7 climbed	12 night-time	17 crimes
3 blind	8 pilot	13 buy	18 shy
4 likes	9 bride	14 sides	19 lie
5 light	10 knife	15 ninth	20 child

9. /əʊ/ *(12)*

¹l	o	a	t	h	e			
o								
a							²w	
f		³l	o	a	⁴n		o	
					⁵o	a	k	
			⁶g		t		e	
		⁷s	t	o	n	e		
⁸h	h	a					⁹t	
o	o	t		¹⁰l			o	
¹¹m	o	w		¹²o	w	n		
e		¹³b	l	o	w		e	

10. /eə/ *(14)*

¹n	i	g	h	t	²m	a	r	e		³s
o					i					q
w			⁴f	a	r	e				u
⁵h	a	i	r							a
e						⁶t		r	
⁷r	e	⁸p	a	i	r		⁹w	h	e	r	e
e		e					e		a	
	¹⁰f	a	i	r		¹¹p	a	i	r	
		r					r			
							¹²s	h	a	r	e

11. /ʃ/ *(15)*

1 If you are anxious about future generations, please give a generous donation to our organisation. We have a special social and educational programme. We also have irrigation and conservation projects, and a programme of vaccination against infectious disease. We need your financial support. We are sure that you will help us take action.

2 There was a lot of shouting at immigration because one of the musicians did not show her identification. The official did not believe her explanation and refused her permission to enter the station.

3 The ambi<u>ti</u>ous language learner, who wants to do some trans<u>l</u>a<u>ti</u>on after gradua<u>ti</u>on, <u>sh</u>ould work hard on pronuncia<u>ti</u>on and dicta<u>ti</u>on as well as conversa<u>ti</u>on.

4 The exhibi<u>ti</u>on which opens tomorrow reflects the pa<u>ss</u>ion of one man. After years of explora<u>ti</u>on into this an<u>ci</u>ent civilisa<u>ti</u>on, Dr Igna<u>ti</u>ous brings us his impre<u>ss</u>ions of Gre<u>ci</u>an life.

12. /f/ (16)

2 a. philanthropist
b. pharmacist
c. philosophy
d. photography
e. anglophile
f. telephone
g. telegraph
h. phonemes
i. arachnophobia
j. physics

13. Final c or ic (17)

1 musical	**7** mechanically
2 panicker	**8** automatically
3 critical	**9** trafficker
4 picnicking	**10** systematically
5 electrical	**11** mimicking
6 basically	

14. Final /k/ (18)

1 walk park	**8** work sick	**15** truck
2 headache	**9** luck	**16** talk
3 socks	**10** basic	**17** joke
4 forks	**11** make mistakes	**18** sticks
5 elastic	**12** drink	**19** unique
6 back book	**13** think bike	**20** historic
7 bake cake	**14** neck	

15. Final /tʃ/ (19)

1 pitch church	**6** fetch match
2 torch	**7** touch branch
3 coach reached	**8** patch ditch
4 watch	**9** preached
5 beach	**10** bunch/Finch

16. Adding endings to final y (20)

								¹f	a	c	t	o	r	i	e	²s
								e								t
					³w	o	r	r	i	e	s					u
							r				⁴m					d
	⁵s	⁶t	o	r	i	e	⁷s				o					i
		r			e		a				n					e
		i			s		y				k					s
⁸l	i	e	s				⁹s	p	i	e	s					
o		s									y				¹⁰	
r				¹¹d	o	n	¹²k	e	y	s					e	
¹³r							e								n	
i			¹⁴p	l	a	y	s								j	
e							s								o	
¹⁵s	t	o	r	e	y	s			¹⁶f	l	i	e	s		y	

17. Endings able and ible (22)

1 preferable	**7** comfortable
2 profitable	**8** unbelievable
3 personable	**9** possible
4 terrible	**10** usable
5 drinkable	**11** indigestible
6 manageable	**12** acceptable

18. Endings ise and ize (24)

1 prize
2 apologise/apologize
3 advertising
4 advised exercise
5 sympathise/sympathize
6 surprise
7 criticising/criticizing
8 size
9 wise
10 realised/realized

19. Endings s and es (25)

1
a. watches	g. companies
b. finds	h. workers
c. helps	i. misses
d. thinks	j. says
e. cities	k. wishes
f. taxes	l. books studies

2 My brother David lives in Sydney where he *works* for a Japanese computer company. They make office machines such as *typewriters* and word processors. He deals with the workers' pay and conditions.

His wife Sandy is a nurse who helps old people. Sometimes she *visits* them in their homes and sometimes she takes them to the hospital. Their daughter Zoe is seven *years* old. She goes to school every day but when she comes home she likes playing with the dog and cat. After she *finishes* her homework she usually watches TV.

On Sundays my brother *plays* hockey. Sometimes Sandy, Zoe and the dog go to watch one of his *matches*. Afterwards David drives to one of the *beaches* nearby. Everybody swims except for the dog who runs along the sand and *barks* at the waves. Sometimes Zoe thinks she is a dog too and *copies* him until my brother gets angry and shouts at them both to stop.

20. Irregular plurals (27)

I
1 – e. thieves   4 – c. shelves
2 – a. knives   5 – b. wives
3 – d. leaves   6 – f. loaves
                 7 – g. calves

2
a. teeth toothbrush
b. mouse mice
c. foot feet

3 potatoes tomatoes heroes

4
a. potatoes   d. heroes   g. videos
b. portfolios   e. tomatoes   h. cameos
c. radios   f. pianos   i. solos

21. Adding suffixes to words ending in e (28)

I
type – typed typing typist
write – writing writer
come – coming comer comely
telephone – telephoned telephoning telephonist
notice – noticed noticing noticeable
face – faced facing faceless
encourage – encouraged encouraging encouragement
change – changed changing changeable changeless
value – valued valuing valuable valuer valueless
argue – argued arguing arguable argument
free – freed freeing freer freely
disagree – disagreed disagreeing disagreeable disagreement

2 I am writing to thank you for having us to stay and to let you know that the improvements on our house have now been completed and hopefully we can move in very soon. We are driving there next Saturday. The children are extremely excited about living in such a beautiful house, but I'm a little worried about keeping the valuable furniture safely away from them!

Hoping you'll be coming to visit us soon.

Yours truly

3
a. changeable   f. aging
b. courageous   g. deciding
c. seeing   h. likely
d. disagreement   i. calculations
e. knowledgeable

22. Adding suffixes to one-syllable words ending in a consonant (31)

I
a. wetter   g. sleeping
b. waiting   h. shopping
c. weeding   i. fatter
d. wedding   j. slimming
e. hottest   k. thinner
f. hooted

23. Adding suffixes to multi-syllable words ending in a consonant (32)

I
a. occurred mattered development
b. regretted profited benefited
c. referred permitted
d. preferred

2
1 – h. inherited wealth
2 – f. banqueting hall
3 – d. pensioner
4 – b. marketing department
5 – c. deferred payment
6 – a. ironing board
7 – i. dieting programme
8 – g. limited edition

24. Adding suffixes to words ending in l (34)

I
a. equalled   d. fatally
b. labelled   e. cancellation
c. propeller

2
a. boiled   e. feeling
b. quarrelling   f. excellent
c. killed   g. counsellor
d. failed   h. controlled

25. Adding ly to form adverbs *(35)*

1
a. correctly	f. electrically
b. completely	g. attractively
c. inexpensively	h. falsely
d. unhappily	i. normally
e. ably	j. immediately

2 (Possible answers)
a. quietly calmly lazily
b. sweetly loudly softly
c. busily carefully angrily
d. hungrily quickly healthily
e. politely rudely warmly
f. kindly angrily sadly

26. Homophones *(37)*

Dear Jim

Here I am in Alaska. I've been here for two weeks now and I can't bear the thought of going home. You can see our house in the photograph – it's right next to the sea. The waves break on the beach just in front of the windows. When it's stormy, they look like the manes or tails of white horses. The huge wood behind the house is full of deer, hares and bears, and you can walk there for miles and not meet anyone. You can really believe old stories of black magic and witches. The peace in the evening is wonderful – it is so silent. I go up the stairs and sew or read for hours and all I can hear is the sea.

Would you like to come and stay? The air fare is really not very expensive. Hope to see you soon.

Love

Jennifer

Part 2

1. Letters of the alphabet *(38)*

1

1	2	3	4	5	6	7
/eɪ/	/iː/	/e/	/aɪ/	/əʊ/	/uː/	/aː/
a	b	f	i	o	q	r
h	c	l	y		u	
j	d	m			w	
k	e	n				
	g	s				
	p	x				
	t	z				
	v					

2
a. VAT	f. GMT	k. BBC	p. LSD
b. USA	g. IOU	l. ITV	q. NB
c. BA	h. GB	m. VSO	r. PTO
d. CIA	i. UK	n. AD	s. RSVP
e. HQ	j. B&B	o. EC	t. PhD

2. Initial a *(40)*

1
Group A
a. actually
b. average
c. accident
d. age
e. aspirin

Group B
a. apart
b. announced
c. affair
d. airport
e. attend

Group C
a. arrange
b. among
c. away
d. always
e. agree

Group D
a. adult
b. accent
c. afford
d. album
e. angry

2 A age /eɪ/ /æ/
   B airport /eə/ /ə/
   C always /ɔː/ /ə/
   D afford /ə/ /æ/

3. Initial e *(42)*

1 a. educate   d. empty
   b. elbow   e. elephant
   c. eleven   f. engine

2 elbow empty engine educate elephant

3 eleven

4 **Group A**
   a. entire
   b. enter
   c. end

   Group B
   a. elder
   b. elect
   c. electric

   Group C
   a. excite
   b. exchange
   c. excellent

   Group D
   a. experiment
   b. expensive
   c. exercise

5 A entire /ɪ/ /e/
   B elder /e/ /ɪ/
   C excellent /e/ /ɪ/
   D exercise /e/ /ɪ/

4. Initial i *(44)*

1 a. island   e. initials
   b. ice   f. ink
   c. inch   g. invitation
   d. inn   h. iron

2 ink inn initials invitation inch

3 ice iron island

4 **Group A**
a. immense
b. imprison
c. idea

   Group B
a. idle
b. identify
c. inside

   Group C
a. icy
b. ill
c. India

5 A /idea /aɪ/ /ɪ/
   B inside /ɪ/ /aɪ/
   C icy /aɪ/ /ɪ/

5. Initial o *(45)*

1 a. occupy   2 /ɒ/
   b. often   /ɒ/
   c. opera   /ɒ/
   d. offend   /ə/
   e. observe   /ə/
   f. obtain   /ə/
   g. obedient   /ə/
   h. occupation /ɒ/
   i. obscure   /ə/
   j. opposition /ɒ/
   k. ox   /ɒ/

6. Initial u *(46)*

1 a. umbrella   d. uniform
   b. unicorn   e. upstairs
   c. unhappy   f. unicycle

2 umbrella unhappy upstairs

3 unicycle uniform unicorn

4 **Group A**
a. useless
b. upset
c. uphill

   Group B
a. union
b. unique
c. unable

   Group C
a. uncommon
b. underline
c. unisex

5 A useless /juː/ /ʌ/
   B unable /ʌ/ /juː/
   C unisex /juː/ /ʌ/

7. c *(48)*

I

a. /k/ /s/	g. /s/
b. /k/ /s/	h. /ʃ/
c. /s/ /s/	i. /k/ /s/ /k/
d. /s/	j. /k/ /k/
e. /k/ /s/	k. /ʃ/
f. /k/ /s/	l. /k/ /s/

2 **Group A**
a. twice
b. juice
c. decide

Group B
a. balcony
b. car
c. anchor

Group C
a. proficiency
b. sufficient
c. efficient

Group D
a. accident
b. accelerate
c. successful

3 A /s/
B /k/
C /ʃ/
D /k/ + /s/

8. ch *(50)*

I

	2	
a. butcher		/tʃ/
b. architect		/k/
c. headaches		/k/
d. kitchen		/tʃ/
e. moustache		/ʃ/
f. chauffeur		/ʃ/
g. lunch		/tʃ/
h. chemist		/k/
i. champion		/tʃ/
j. chefs		/ʃ/
k. sketch		/tʃ/
i. choose		/tʃ/

9. ea *(51)*

I

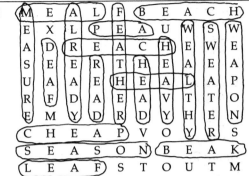

2

a. meal	f. sweater	k. reach	p. feather
b. deaf	g. weapon	l. cheap	q. wealthy
c. measure	h. pea	m. beak	r. head
d. beach	i. already	n. leaf	s. heal
e. season	j. heavy	o. read	

10. ear *(53)*

I **Group A**
a. gears
b. clear
c. search

Group B
a. earnest
b. Earth
c. beard

Group C
a. years
b. hear
c. earthquake

Group D
a. nearly
b. pear
c. rear

2 A search /ɜː/ /ɪə/
B beard /ɪə/ /ɜː/
C earthquake /ɜː/ /ɪə/
D pear /eə/ /ɪə/

II. ei *(54)*

I veils
2 freight
3 weight
4 eighty
5 reign
6 height
7 foreign
8 leisure
9 neighbour
I0 vein

12. g *(55)*

1 Group A
a. fridge
b. bargain
c. legs
d. guilty

Group B
a. angry
b. cage
c. huge
d. oxygen

Group C
a. bridge
b. badge
c. agree
d. vegetables

2 A fridge /dʒ/ /g/
B angry /g/ /dʒ/
C agree /g/ /dʒ/

13. ie *(57)*

1 Group A
a. scientist
b. diet
c. society
d. ancient

Group B
a. audience
b. experience
c. twentieth
d. impatience

Group C
a. niece
b. relief
c. series
d. review

Group D
a. friendship
b. conscience
c. efficient
d. proficiency

2 A ancient /ə/ /aɪə/
B impatience /ə/ ɪə/
C review /juː/ /iː/
D friendship /e/ /ə/

14. ng *(58)*

1 a. finger   d. hangar
b. wrong   e. messenger
c. king

2 Group A
a. long
b. ringing
c. sting
d. change

Group B
a. hungry
b. strongest
c. danger
d. longer

Group C
a. belong
b. young
c. wrong
d. stranger

3 A change /ndʒ/ /ŋ/
B danger /ndʒ/ /ŋg/
C stranger /ndʒ/ /ŋ/

15. oa *(60)*

1 a. foal   f. oar
b. soap   g. goat
c. coat   h. goal
d. oak   i. loaf
e. toast

2 oar /ɔː/

3 Group A
a. abroad
b. blackboard
c. approach

Group B
a. broadcast
b. boast
c. load

Group C
a. cardboard
b. loan
c. roast

4 A approach /əʊ/ /ɔː/
B broadcast /ɔː/ /əʊ/
C cardboard /ɔː/ /əʊ/

16. oo *(61)*

1 a. bookshelf   d. moon
b. football   e. cooker
c. school   f. pool

2 bookshelf football cooker

3 moon pool school

4 Group A
  a. wool
  b. hood
  c. goose

Group B
  a. noon
  b. tool
  c. cook

Group C
  a. shoot
  b. tooth
  c. hook

5 A goose /uː/ /ʊ/
    B cook /ʊ/ /uː/
    C hook /ʊ/ /uː/

17. or (63)

1 a. equator   d. orchestra
    b. organ   e. cork
    c. forty   f. anchor

2 orchestra organ forty cork

3 anchor equator

4 a. work   **5** /ɜː/
    b. more   /ɔː/
    c. forest   /ɒ/
    d. horrible   /ɒ/
    e. border   /ɔː/
    f. correct   /ə/
    g. order   /ɔː/
    h. sailor   /ə/
    i. world   /ɜː/

18. ou (64)

1 a. mountain   f. mouse
    b. mouth   g. cloud
    c. soup   h. souvenir
    d. couple   i. fountain
    e. pound

2 souvenir soup

3 couple

4 **Group A**
    a. count
    b. south
    c. route

Group B
  a. countries
  b. cousins
  c. lounge

Group C
  a. account
  b. sound
  c. double

Group D
  a. wound
  b. through
  c. loud

5 A route /uː/ /aʊ/
    B lounge /aʊ/ /ʌ/
    C double /ʌ/ /aʊ/
    D loud /aʊ/ /uː/

19. ough (66)

A cruise

The wind got up, the sea got *rough*
And very soon we'd had *enough*
Some caught colds and started to *cough*
We just wanted to get off.
The captain said we must be *tough*
Sailors are of stronger stuff.

But then at last the sun came *through*
And then we felt as good as new.
Just two more days to get to port
We packed the presents that we'd *bought*
We sighted land, a horse and a *plough*
Nearly home, we were happy now.

20. our (67)

1

a. court	**2**	/ɔː/
b. tourist		/ʊe/
c. sour		/aʊə/
d. yours		/ɔː/
e. four		/ɔː/
f. resource		/ɔː/
g. source		/ɔː/
h. hour		/aʊə/
i. neighbour		/ə/

21. ow *(68)*

I   a. arrow
   b. shower
   c. tower
   d. crown
   e. bowl
   f. snow

2   crown shower tower

3   bowl arrow snow

4   **Group A**
   a. cow
   b. now
   c. low

   Group B
   a. sorrow
   b. yellow
   c. allow

   Group C
   a. own
   b. drown
   c. town

   Group D
   a. power
   b. mow
   c. flower

5   a. low /əʊ/ /aʊ/
   b. allow /aʊ/ /əʊ/
   c. own /əʊ/ /aʊ/
   d. mow /əʊ/ /aʊ/

22. qu(e) *(70)*

I

/kw/		/k/
question	squeeze	unique
frequent	equal	antique
square	quarrel	
request	quarter	

   a. square
   b. equal
   c. question
   d. quarters
   e. antique
   f. request
   g. squeeze
   h. quarrel
   i. frequent
   j. unique

23. th *(71)*

I   a. thousand
   b. bath
   c. three
   d. tooth
   e. thermometer
   f. thumb
   g. feather

2   three bath thumb tooth thousand thermometer

3   feather

4   **Group A**
   a. through
   b. thorough
   c. although

   Group B
   a. months
   b. health
   c. with

   Group C
   a. bathroom
   b. weather
   c. rhythm

   Group D
   a. athletics
   b. furthest
   c. gather

5   A although /ð/ /θ/
   B with /ð/ /θ/
   C bathroom /θ/ /ð/
   D athletics /θ/ /ð/

24. Adding e *(73)*

They climbed on up through woods of *pine*
High above the River Rhine.
They'd brought their lunch but not a map,
They'd got some plates but not a *cap*.

The air was cool but the weather was *fine*.
They ate their food and drank their *wine*.
After the meal they thought of a *plan*
To see who was quickest, woman or *man*.

'Get to the bottom as fast as you *can*.'
One, two, three, go, and off they ran.
The man went left and trusted to *fate*
Down a steep path – 'At the bottom, I'll wait'.

He suddenly fell and hit his *shin*.
'If this goes on, I'll never *win*.'
He couldn't walk, he had to *hop*
And every few steps he had to stop.

The woman turned right, and said 'I *hope*
This is the way down the easier slope.'
It started to rain and she hadn't a *hat*.
She wore a small plate and was happy with that.

In the woods in the valley, the sun didn't *shine*.
She looked for her man but there wasn't a sign.
She took out some paper and wrote him a *note*:
'I'm sorry, must go or I'll miss the last boat.'

When the man got there the woman was *not*.
He was weary and wet, and his leg hurt a lot.
'I must exercise more, to be properly fit.
I'll get into trainers and buy all the *kit*.'

The game is all over and the score is one *nil*
But he's still hopping madly around that big *hill*.

25. Final se *(75)*

1
a. pause	g. wise
b. chase	h. promise
c. nose	i. choose
d. goose	j. erase
e. expense	k. course
f. release	l. cheese

2
a. noise	e. bruise
b. blouse	f. mouse
c. purse	g. nurse
d. applause	h. rose

3 bruise noise rose blouse applause

4 mouse nurse purse

26. s and es in plurals and third person verbs *(78)*

1 **Group 1**
add burn baby beer build leave hold door
law need seagull pig meeting swim ring
sell wind record thing programme tree
train turn rain smooth

Group 2
carpet break fork kick jet make plant myth
milk night market start stamp suit week
shape take talk wait proof

Group 3
church cage face garage dress fox pass
nose voice

2 **Group A**
a. cooks
b. asks
c. dogs

Group B
a. students
b. paths
c. heads

Group C
a. jobs
b. babies
c. stops

Group D
a. finishes
b. teaches
c. machines

Group E
a. glasses
b. washes
c. does

Group F
a. writes
b. letters
c. doors

3 a. dogs /z/ /s/
b. heads /z/ /s/
c. stops /s/ /z/
d. machines /z/ /ɪz/
e. does /z/ /ɪz/
f. writes /s/ /z/

27. Final y *(81)*

1
Babies *cry*
Children ask *why*
Kids are *shy*
Parents *try*
And in *my* life
The years *fly by*

2 To *apply* for the job which will be vacant in
July, you first need to *qualify* as a teacher.

28. Past endings *(82)*

1 **Unvoiced sounds**: approach attack bath
cough crash cross dance drop fetch hope
jump laugh like notice pack promise reach
relax shop walk wash

/d/ or /t/: accept act add attend attract avoid
connect defend demand depend educate
excite fold mend persuade start visit

Vowel sounds: admire agree allow answer
appear argue compare continue deliver
destroy die empty enjoy enter follow
hire play pour remember repair reply
show

Voiced sounds: arrive bathe call climb
clothe control describe disturb drag
explain fail frighten imagine improve
inform join love manage name organise
pull receive rub

29. Shifting stress in two-syllable words *(84)*

1 a.	2 b.	13 a.	14 b.	25 a.	26 b.
3 b.	4 a.	15 b.	16 a.	27 b.	28 a.
5 a.	6 b.	17 b.	18 a.	29 b.	30 a.
7 b.	8 a.	19 a.	20 b.	31 b.	32 a.
9 a.	10 b.	21 a.	22 b.	33 a.	34 b.
11 b.	12 a.	23 a.	24 b.		

30. Silent letters *(86)*

1
a. Psychology	k. hymn
b. honest	l. pneumonia
c. Whose	m. whole
d. knee	n. hour
e. bomb	o. Who
f. gnat	p. wrong
g. ghost	q. climb
h. know knitting	r. psychopath
i. knock	s. wrap
j. knowledge	t. knot

2
a. half listen	k. palm
b. castle night	l. calm flight
c. receipt	m. sword
d. doubt	n. Science
e. talked walked	o. government
f. handkerchiefs Christmas	p. exhaust vehicle
g. Wednesday sandwich	q. iron
h. chalk cupboard	r. stalks
i. answer	s. folk-songs
j. muscles	t. debts

31. Silent syllables *(88)*

1 fav<u>ou</u>rite op<u>e</u>ra

2 av<u>e</u>rage nati<u>o</u>nal temp<u>e</u>rature mod<u>e</u>rate

3 cam<u>e</u>ra

4 Hist<u>o</u>ry Capit<u>a</u>lism Machin<u>e</u>ry Bound<u>a</u>ry

5 Ev<u>e</u>ry laund<u>e</u>rette mis<u>e</u>rable

6 myst<u>e</u>ry diff<u>e</u>rent

7 diction<u>a</u>ry hist<u>o</u>ry

8 mission<u>a</u>ry flav<u>ou</u>ring necess<u>a</u>ry cook<u>e</u>ry

9 happ<u>e</u>ning surg<u>e</u>ry

10 gen<u>e</u>ral sev<u>e</u>ral

11 hopef<u>u</u>lly vict<u>o</u>ry

32. Homographs *(89)*

3 a.	**4** b.	**11** a.	**12** b.
5 b.	**6** a.	**13** b.	**14** a.
7 b.	**8** a.	**15** b.	**16** a.
9 a.	**10** b.	**17** b.	**18** a.